Table of Contents

Introduction 5
The Significance of Beer in Human History 5
Beer as a Cultural and Social Symbol 9
The Journey of This Book 13

Chapter 1: Mesopotamia: The Birthplace of Beer .. 16
Sumerians and the Hymn to Ninkasi 16
Early Brewing Techniques 20
The Role of Beer in Sumerian Society 24
Beer in Trade and Economy 28

Chapter 2: Egypt: The Nectar of the Pharaohs 32
Ancient Egyptian Brewing Methods 32
The Symbolism of Beer in Egyptian Mythology 37
Beer in Daily Life and Rituals 41
Brewing Innovations in Ancient Egypt 45

Chapter 3: Ancient Europe: Monasteries and Medieval Brews 49
Monastic Brewing Traditions 49
The Monks' Contribution to Beer Production 53
Beer in Medieval Europe 57
The Influence of Monasteries on Modern Brewing 62

Chapter 4: Ancient Asia: Beyond the Cradle of Civilization 66
Chinese and Indian Brewing Traditions 66
Rice, Millet, and Sorghum Brews 71
The Cultural Significance of Beer in Asia 75
Beer Along the Silk Road 79

Chapter 5: Nordic Nectar: Beer in Northern Europe ... 84
Viking Brewing Techniques ... *84*
Beer in Norse Mythology ... *88*
Social and Cultural Role of Beer in the North ... *92*
Viking Beer Expeditions ... *96*

Chapter 6: Beer's Journey Through Time: Innovations and Adaptations ... 100
Brewing Methods Evolve ... *100*
Fermentation Discoveries ... *104*
From Clay Pots to Wooden Barrels ... *108*
The Importance of Beer in Long-Distance Trade ... *112*

Chapter 7: Ancient Brewing Revival: Modern Experiments and Archaeological Revelations ... 116
Rediscovering Ancient Beer Recipes ... *116*
Archaeological Finds and Insights ... *121*
Experimental Archaeology: Reconstructing Ancient Brews ... *125*
The Resurgence of Historical Brewing Techniques ... *129*

Conclusion ... 133
Tracing Beer's Unbroken Thread Through History ... *133*
The Universality of Beer ... *137*
Beer's Continuing Evolution ... *141*

Wordbook ... 146
Supplementary Materials ... 149

Copyright © 2023 by Maxwell J. Aromano (Author)

All rights reserved. No part of this book may be reproduced or utilized in any form or by any means, electronic or mechanical, including photocopying, recording or by any information storage and retrieval system, without permission in writing from the publisher, except for brief quotations in critical articles or reviews.

The content of this book is based on various sources and is intended for educational and entertainment purposes only. While the author has made every effort to ensure the accuracy, completeness, and reliability of the information provided, the information may be subject to errors, omissions, or inaccuracies. Therefore, the author makes no warranties, express or implied, regarding the content of this book.

Readers are advised to seek the guidance of a licensed professional before attempting any techniques or actions outlined in this book. The author is not responsible for any losses, damages, or injuries that may arise from the use of information contained within. The information provided in this book is not intended to be a substitute for professional advice, and readers should not rely solely on the information presented.

By reading this book, readers acknowledge that the author is not providing legal, financial, medical, or professional advice. Any reliance on the information contained in this book is solely at the reader's own risk.

Thank you for selecting this book as a valuable source of knowledge and inspiration. Our aim is to provide you with insights and information that will enrich your understanding and enhance your personal growth. We appreciate your decision to embark on this journey of discovery with us, and we hope that this book will exceed your expectations and leave a lasting impact on your life.

Title: Beer's Ancient Cradle: From Mesopotamia to Monasteries

Subtitle: Exploring the Origins and Rituals of Humanity's Favorite Brew

Series: Ale Ages: Tracing the Timeline of Beer
Author: Maxwell J. Aromano

Introduction

The Significance of Beer in Human History

Throughout the annals of human history, few beverages have held a place as venerable and cherished as beer. It is more than just a simple drink; it is a testament to human ingenuity, an embodiment of cultural diversity, and a reflection of the human desire for social connection and recreation. In this introductory chapter, we embark on a journey to explore the profound significance of beer in shaping the human experience.

A Liquid Tapestry of Human Culture

Beer is more than just a liquid that quenches thirst; it is a living testament to the evolution of human society. From the earliest civilizations in Mesopotamia and Egypt to the bustling craft breweries of the modern age, beer has been woven into the fabric of our cultures, reflecting the values, beliefs, and rituals of each era.

Mesopotamia, often referred to as the cradle of civilization, offers us the earliest known evidence of beer production. The Sumerians, a people who called this fertile land their home, not only brewed beer but also immortalized their brewing process in the Hymn to Ninkasi. In their words, we see the reverence they held for this amber elixir, recognizing it as a symbol of divine creation and a cornerstone of their society.

Egypt, the land of the pharaohs, provides another remarkable chapter in the story of beer. Here, beer wasn't just a beverage; it was a source of nutrition, a currency of trade, and a vital component of religious rituals. The ancient Egyptians believed that beer was a gift from the gods, and its production was entrusted to priestly brewers who channeled their spiritual connection into every brew.

Beyond Nourishment: The Social and Ritualistic Role of Beer

Beer is more than just sustenance; it has long held a central role in the social and spiritual lives of communities worldwide. It is the bridge that brings people together, fostering camaraderie, celebration, and storytelling.

In medieval Europe, for instance, beer was a staple at monasteries, where monks crafted complex brews not only for their own nourishment but also as a means of sustenance for travelers and pilgrims. Beer, in this context, transcended its nutritional value to symbolize hospitality and generosity.

Moreover, beer has played a pivotal role in various religious and cultural rituals. In the ancient world, libations of beer were poured to honor deities, and it was believed that sharing a drink could forge bonds between humans and gods. Such rituals continue today, whether it's the communal toasts during festivals in Germany, the sake ceremonies in Japan, or the craft beer tastings at modern breweries.

Beer as a Mirror to Humanity's Inventive Spirit

The history of beer is also a testament to human inventiveness. Brewing has evolved from crude methods using clay pots and rudimentary fermentation techniques to the precision and innovation seen in today's craft beer revolution. The story of beer mirrors our ability to adapt, experiment, and refine our practices over millennia.

This book will take you on a chronological journey through time and across cultures, unearthing the stories and innovations that have made beer an enduring and cherished part of the human story. From the early civilizations of Mesopotamia and Egypt to the monastic traditions of medieval Europe and the vibrant craft beer scene of the 21st century, we will trace the threads that have bound beer to our collective history.

In the chapters that follow, we'll explore these pivotal moments and the people who shaped the course of beer's history, offering you a deeper understanding of how this ancient brew has continually adapted, transformed, and remained an integral part of our lives. So, let us raise a metaphorical glass and embark on this remarkable journey through the world of beer, a journey that mirrors the story of humanity itself.

Beer as a Cultural and Social Symbol

Beer is not merely a beverage; it is a multifaceted prism through which we can explore the heart of human culture and the intricacies of our social interactions. From ancient rituals to modern gatherings, beer has been a symbol of celebration, community, and identity. In this section, we will delve deep into the role of beer as a cultural and social symbol, transcending its liquid form to become a mirror of our values and aspirations.

A Symbol of Celebration

Beer has long held a place at the center of celebrations and festivities, acting as an emblem of joy and revelry. In cultures across the world, it has been the libation of choice during weddings, festivals, and communal gatherings. The act of raising a glass, clinking it with others, and sharing a toast is a universal expression of celebration and camaraderie.

In ancient Egypt, beer was integral to celebrations honoring the gods and the Pharaohs. Its consumption was seen as an act of reverence and gratitude, symbolizing the joy of life and the divine blessings bestowed upon the people.

In Medieval Europe, especially within the monastic communities, beer was brewed with meticulous care and shared generously with travelers, weary pilgrims, and fellow monks. It was not merely a means of nourishment but also a symbol of the monastic commitment to hospitality and charity.

The Social Glue

Beer has a remarkable capacity to dissolve social barriers, bringing people from diverse backgrounds together. Pubs, taverns, and beer gardens have served as egalitarian meeting places where individuals from all walks of life can gather, converse, and connect.

In the United Kingdom, the pub has been the cornerstone of social life for centuries. It's a place where people come not just to enjoy a pint but also to engage in conversation, celebrate victories, and seek solace during times of sorrow. The pub is where communities form and friendships are forged, and it often serves as an anchor in rapidly changing times.

In Germany, beer gardens have been an integral part of the culture for generations. Families, friends, and strangers come together under the shade of chestnut trees to share communal tables, laughter, and, of course, excellent beer. This tradition epitomizes the idea that beer can be a powerful force for bringing people together.

Identity and Expression

Beer is a canvas upon which cultures paint their unique identities and stories. Different regions and communities have developed their distinct brewing traditions, flavors, and rituals, creating a tapestry of diversity in the world of beer.

Belgium, for instance, is renowned for its complex and diverse array of beer styles, each with its own history and character. From Trappist ales brewed by monks to lambics aged in open vats, Belgian beer is a reflection of the nation's commitment to preserving tradition while embracing innovation.

Japan offers a fascinating example of how beer can be intertwined with cultural identity. Here, traditional sake brewing techniques have influenced the production of rice-based beers, resulting in a harmonious fusion of ancient and modern flavors.

Beer and the Passage of Time

Throughout history, beer has been a witness to the ebb and flow of human civilization. It has been there during times of jubilation and sorrow, war and peace, tradition and change. It is an enduring symbol of our capacity to adapt, create, and connect across the boundaries of time and culture.

As we journey through the chapters of this book, we will uncover the intricate stories that beer tells about our past and the powerful role it continues to play in our present. It's a reminder that, in the midst of our ever-evolving world, some traditions remain constant, and beer, as both a cultural and social symbol, endures as a cherished companion on our collective journey.

The Journey of This Book

As we embark on this historical exploration of beer, it is essential to understand the path we are about to traverse. In these pages, we will journey through time, crisscrossing continents, and immersing ourselves in the rich tapestry of beer's history. This chapter sets the stage for the captivating voyage ahead, giving you a roadmap of the chapters and themes that will unfold.

Following the Unbroken Thread

Our journey begins in the ancient cradle of beer, Mesopotamia. Here, in the land between the Tigris and Euphrates rivers, the Sumerians composed the Hymn to Ninkasi, a poetic ode to the art of brewing. This hymn not only provides a glimpse into the earliest known brewing techniques but also illustrates the profound cultural and spiritual significance of beer.

From Mesopotamia, we will cross the sands of time to ancient Egypt, where beer flowed as freely as the Nile. In this chapter, we will explore the role of beer in Egyptian daily life, its connection to myth and royalty, and the secrets of ancient Egyptian brewing methods.

Our journey then takes us to the heart of medieval Europe, where monasteries became bastions of brewing excellence. Monks, often dismissed as ascetics, played a pivotal role in refining brewing techniques and preserving the art during turbulent times. We'll uncover the sacred and secular aspects of beer within monastic walls.

Venturing further east, we'll arrive in ancient Asia. Here, beer takes on a different form, utilizing ingredients like rice, millet, and sorghum. Chinese and Indian brewing traditions offer a fascinating contrast to their Western counterparts, revealing the versatility of beer as a global beverage.

Northern Europe beckons us next, where the Vikings and Norse mythology intertwine with beer's story. In the cold northern climes, beer served as sustenance, a social lubricant, and a window into the realms of gods and legends. This chapter will shed light on Viking brewing techniques and the role of beer in Norse culture.

Innovations, Adaptations, and Trade

Our voyage through time then turns to the evolution of beer itself. In "Beer's Journey Through Time," we will witness the metamorphosis of brewing methods, fermentation discoveries, and the shift from clay pots to wooden barrels. This chapter highlights how beer's adaptability and innovation have allowed it to withstand the test of time.

With the chapter "Ancient Brewing Revival," we leap forward to modern times. Here, we will delve into the resurgence of historical brewing techniques, where archaeologists, historians, and passionate brewers join forces to rediscover ancient beer recipes, uncover archaeological finds, and engage in experimental archaeology.

Tracing the Threads of Beer's History

Finally, in the concluding chapter, "Tracing Beer's Unbroken Thread Through History," we will bring our journey full circle. We will reflect on the universal nature of beer, its continuing evolution, and the enduring legacy of a beverage that has transcended millennia.

As we travel from ancient Mesopotamia to the present day, it is our hope that this book will not only provide you with a comprehensive understanding of beer's history but also ignite your own appreciation for this remarkable beverage. Beer is more than a mere drink; it is a time capsule, a cultural touchstone, and a symbol of our shared human experience. So, let us embark on this journey together, raising a metaphorical glass to the enduring legacy of beer as it flows through the pages of history.

Chapter 1: Mesopotamia: The Birthplace of Beer
Sumerians and the Hymn to Ninkasi

In the fertile crescent of Mesopotamia, where the Tigris and Euphrates rivers cradled the birth of human civilization, beer made its illustrious debut. It was here, amidst the ancient Sumerians, that beer was not just brewed; it was venerated as a divine elixir, an integral part of daily life, and a medium for recording history and culture.

A Glimpse into the Past: Sumerian Civilization

To understand the significance of beer in Sumeria, we must first step back in time to the third millennium BCE, where the Sumerians thrived in the region known as the "land between the rivers." These ancient people were pioneers in various fields, from agriculture to writing, and their innovations laid the groundwork for future societies.

Sumerian Society: Sumer was composed of city-states like Ur, Uruk, and Eridu, each with its own unique character and governance. These city-states boasted monumental ziggurats, advanced irrigation systems, and a highly stratified society where priests and rulers held significant power.

Cuneiform Writing: Perhaps the most profound contribution of the Sumerians was the invention of cuneiform writing. They etched symbols into clay tablets, creating the earliest known written language. This innovation allowed them to record not only economic transactions and administrative details but also stories, myths, and, importantly for our journey, recipes.

The Hymn to Ninkasi: Ode to Beer Brewing

One of the most remarkable pieces of Sumerian literature that has survived the ravages of time is the Hymn to Ninkasi. This hymn is far more than a simple recipe for brewing beer; it is a poetic masterpiece that serves as a window into the soul of Sumerian culture and their deep reverence for beer.

Ninkasi: Before delving into the hymn itself, we must meet its protagonist, Ninkasi. In Sumerian mythology, Ninkasi was the goddess of beer, and she was revered as the matron of brewing. Her name itself is a homage to her role, as "Nin" means "lady" and "kasi" means "beer."

The Poetic Elegance: The Hymn to Ninkasi is not a dry set of instructions but a lyrical ode to the art of brewing. It celebrates Ninkasi's birth, her divine role in brewing, and her teachings to humanity. The hymn is structured in a manner that helps the reader visualize the brewing process, from the preparation of bread (a key ingredient) to the fermentation of the beer.

Cultural Significance: The hymn's existence reflects the profound cultural and religious significance of beer in Sumeria. Beer was not just a drink; it was a gift from the gods, an embodiment of the divine. Brewing was a sacred task, and the hymn elevated it to a spiritual practice. The Sumerians believed that Ninkasi's guidance was essential for a successful brew, and her wisdom was passed down through generations.

The Brewing Process: Within the hymn, the brewing process is described in intricate detail. It begins with the baking of bread, which is then crumbled and mixed with water. This mixture, called "bappir," forms the base for the beer. It's a testament to the Sumerians' mastery of fermentation, showcasing their understanding of yeast's role in transforming the mixture into beer.

Beer in Everyday Life: The hymn also provides glimpses into how beer was used in everyday life. It was a staple in the Sumerian diet, offering nourishment and hydration. It was served at feasts, gatherings, and religious ceremonies, uniting the community in joy and reverence.

The Legacy of the Hymn to Ninkasi

The Hymn to Ninkasi is not just a historical relic but a living testament to the enduring connection between humanity and beer. It illustrates how beer transcended its role as a mere beverage to become a cultural touchstone, a religious symbol, and a cornerstone of Sumerian identity.

In the chapters that follow, we will continue our journey through Mesopotamia, exploring early brewing techniques, the role of beer in Sumerian society, and its impact on trade and economy. As we delve deeper into this ancient civilization's relationship with beer, we will uncover the intricate web of culture, religion, and daily life that this amber elixir wove into the fabric of Sumerian existence.

Early Brewing Techniques

In the heart of ancient Mesopotamia, where the Tigris and Euphrates rivers nurtured the cradle of civilization, the art of brewing beer was born. As we delve deeper into this chapter, we step back in time to explore the brewing techniques employed by the pioneering Sumerians. These early methods not only laid the foundation for the brewing traditions we know today but also provide a fascinating glimpse into the ingenuity of our ancestors.

Ingredients of Antiquity

The first and foremost aspect of brewing in ancient Mesopotamia was the selection of ingredients. While modern brewers have access to a wide array of hops, malted barley, and specialized yeast strains, the Sumerians worked with a more limited palette.

Barley: Barley was the primary grain of choice for the Sumerians. It was readily available in the region and well-suited to the brewing process. However, unlike today's malted barley, Sumerians used a precursor known as "emmer wheat," which was malted to create the necessary enzymes for fermentation.

Water: Water was a crucial component, as it formed the base of the beer. The availability and quality of water would have a significant impact on the final brew. The

Sumerians often sourced their water from the Tigris and Euphrates rivers, which had a consistent supply of freshwater.

Bread: Perhaps one of the most unique ingredients in early brewing was bread. The Sumerians made bread from barley and other grains, and it played a vital role in the brewing process. The bread was crumbled and combined with water to create a mash, serving as the source of fermentable sugars for the beer.

Spices and Additives: While the core ingredients were barley, water, and bread, Sumerians also used various spices and additives to flavor and preserve their brews. These included coriander, cumin, and myrtle.

The Brewing Process

The brewing process in ancient Sumeria was a meticulous and labor-intensive affair, reflecting the cultural significance of beer in their society. While the basic principles of fermentation were understood, the techniques used were quite different from modern brewing.

Malting: The process began with the malting of emmer wheat. The grains were soaked in water, allowed to sprout, and then dried. This malting process activated enzymes in the grain that would later break down starches into fermentable sugars during mashing.

Mashing: The crumbled bread was mixed with the malted grain and water, creating a thick, porridge-like mixture known as "bappir." This mash was then heated, allowing the enzymes from the malted grain to convert the starches from the bread into sugars. The result was a sugary liquid called "sikaru."

Fermentation: Once the sugary liquid was separated from the solid remnants of the mash, it was transferred to fermentation vessels. These early brewers likely used large clay pots or fermenting jars. Fermentation was driven by wild yeast present in the environment, which would have resulted in a more spontaneous and less controlled process compared to modern brewing.

Storage: After fermentation, the beer was stored in clay containers. These vessels provided a cool and stable environment for the beer to mature. It's worth noting that, unlike modern brewing, the concept of bottling and sealing beer did not exist at this time.

The Artistry of Ancient Brewing

While the brewing techniques of ancient Mesopotamia may seem rudimentary by modern standards, they were the result of careful observation and refinement. Sumerian brewers possessed a deep understanding of the fermentation process and the critical role of each ingredient.

The beer produced in these early days was not only a source of nourishment but also a symbol of the Sumerian spirit. It was a testament to their ability to harness the resources of their environment and transform them into a beverage that could be enjoyed by all.

In the chapters that follow, we will continue our journey through Mesopotamia, exploring the role of beer in Sumerian society, its significance in trade and economy, and its place in the broader cultural and spiritual landscape. These early brewing techniques were just the beginning of a journey that would span centuries and continents, shaping the history of beer as we know it today.

The Role of Beer in Sumerian Society

In the heart of ancient Mesopotamia, where the Tigris and Euphrates rivers nourished the cradle of civilization, beer held a place of profound importance. It was more than just a beverage; it was a cornerstone of Sumerian society, an essential element of daily life, and a symbol of their connection to the divine. In this section, we delve into the role of beer in Sumerian society, exploring how this amber elixir permeated every aspect of their culture.

Beer as Nourishment and Sustenance

In the Sumerian world, beer was not merely a drink to be enjoyed for leisure; it was a fundamental source of sustenance. The brewing process itself contributed to the transformation of raw ingredients into a nutritious and easily digestible foodstuff.

Liquid Bread: The brewing process, which included the use of malted barley and bread, resulted in a beverage that was akin to liquid bread. It was not just refreshing but also nourishing, providing essential carbohydrates and calories to the Sumerian diet.

Nutritional Value: The nutritional value of beer was especially crucial in a society heavily reliant on agricultural labor. Workers in the fields would consume beer during breaks to replenish their energy, stave off hunger, and remain hydrated in the harsh Mesopotamian climate.

Daily Rations: Beer was often part of the daily rations allocated to laborers, reflecting its status as a basic dietary staple. These rations were often distributed by the authorities, underscoring the importance of beer in ensuring a stable and productive workforce.

A Symbol of Hospitality and Generosity

Beyond its nutritional role, beer was a symbol of hospitality and generosity in Sumerian culture. The act of offering beer to guests held deep social significance, emphasizing the importance of communal bonds and goodwill.

Offerings to Deities: Just as beer was shared with guests, it was also offered to deities as a sign of reverence and gratitude. The Sumerians believed that brewing was a divine gift, and the act of presenting beer to the gods was a way to ensure their favor.

Guest-Friendship: Guest-friendship, an important concept in Sumerian society, was often sealed with the exchange of beer. When two individuals became guest-friends, they would share a drink of beer, signifying their mutual trust and commitment to one another.

Beer and the Divine

The Sumerians had a deep spiritual connection to beer, seeing it as a gift from the gods. Beer was not only consumed in religious rituals but was also believed to possess inherent divine qualities.

Ninkasi's Blessings: As the goddess of beer, Ninkasi was revered as the source of brewing knowledge. The Hymn to Ninkasi celebrated her teachings and wisdom, emphasizing the belief that successful brewing was guided by the divine.

Ritual Libations: Beer was a common offering to gods and goddesses in Sumerian religious ceremonies. Libations of beer were poured onto altars as a gesture of devotion and a means of establishing communication between humans and the divine.

A Unifying Force

Beer was more than just a beverage; it was a social glue that bound the diverse people of Sumeria together. It played a pivotal role in communal gatherings, celebrations, and even conflict resolution.

Feasts and Gatherings: Beer was a staple at Sumerian feasts and gatherings, where it fostered camaraderie and relaxation. These gatherings were vital for building and maintaining social bonds.

Conflict Resolution: In Sumerian legal and social customs, sharing a drink of beer was a way to resolve disputes and conflicts. The act of coming together over a drink symbolized a commitment to finding common ground and peace.

Conclusion: Beer as a Pillar of Sumerian Civilization

In the annals of history, few beverages have left as indelible a mark as beer did on Sumerian society. It was a source of sustenance, a symbol of hospitality, a conduit to the divine, and a unifying force. The Sumerians' reverence for beer was not merely a cultural quirk; it was a reflection of their understanding of its profound role in their civilization.

As we continue our journey through Mesopotamia in the following chapters, we will explore how beer evolved and its impact on trade and economy. The story of beer in this ancient cradle is far from complete, and it is one that intertwines with the very essence of human existence in this remarkable time and place.

Beer in Trade and Economy

In the ancient world of Mesopotamia, beer was not only a vital part of daily life but also played a significant role in the region's trade and economy. The amber elixir brewed from barley, water, and bread was a currency of its own, connecting people, fueling commerce, and shaping economic systems in ways that reverberate even today.

The Birth of a Commodity

Beer's transformation into a commodity began within the household. Brewing beer was a common practice in Sumerian households, with each family brewing their own unique variations. As the brewing process evolved and became more standardized, beer production expanded beyond the home and into larger communal breweries.

Communal Breweries: Communal breweries in Sumerian city-states became hubs for brewing and distributing beer. These breweries were often managed by the temples and employed both skilled brewers and laborers. The beer produced in these establishments was intended for both local consumption and trade.

Early Supply Chains: With the emergence of communal breweries, we witness the early formation of supply chains. Barley was cultivated in the fields, processed in mills, malted in communal malting facilities, brewed in communal breweries, and finally distributed to the populace. This intricate network laid the foundation for more complex trade systems.

The Role of Beer in Trade

Beer played a pivotal role in trade, acting as both a medium of exchange and a valuable commodity in itself. Its significance in trade can be viewed from several perspectives.

Trade Goods: Beer was often exchanged for other goods and services. Merchants, farmers, and laborers received beer as part of their wages, and it was used in trade between city-states. Its liquidity and widespread acceptance made it a valuable trade good.

Standard of Value: Beer served as a standard of value for other commodities. Prices were often quoted in terms of measures of beer, establishing it as a benchmark for economic transactions.

Trade Routes: The flow of beer also drove the development of trade routes. As beer was brewed in various city-states, it needed to be transported to regions where it was less abundant. This gave rise to trade routes and the movement of beer barrels across Mesopotamia.

Economic Impact

The economic impact of beer extended beyond mere trade. It influenced labor practices, taxation, and even the development of the first accounting systems.

Labor and Wages: Beer was often a component of laborers' wages, illustrating its role as a vital source of nourishment and motivation for the workforce. Some labor contracts specified daily beer rations as part of compensation.

Taxation: Beer was subject to taxation in Sumerian society. The temples, which often managed communal breweries, collected taxes in the form of beer. This revenue helped fund temple operations, including public infrastructure projects and religious activities.

Accounting and Records: The need to account for beer production and distribution led to the development of some of the earliest forms of writing and record-keeping. Clay tablets were used to track beer allocations, serving as precursors to more complex accounting systems.

Beer as a Social Equalizer

One of the unique aspects of beer in ancient Mesopotamia was its role in leveling social hierarchies. Unlike other commodities that were primarily controlled by the elite, beer was widely accessible and could be enjoyed by people from all walks of life.

Taverns and Social Gathering Places: Taverns and social gathering places were open to people of various social strata. Here, individuals could come together over a common love for beer, engage in conversation, and form social bonds.

Guest-Friendship: Beer played a significant role in the establishment of guest-friendships, a practice where individuals shared a drink of beer to solidify their friendship. These bonds transcended social divisions and could be forged between people of different social standings.

Conclusion: Beer's Impact on Mesopotamian Economy

In the complex tapestry of ancient Mesopotamia, beer emerged as not only a staple of sustenance but also a dynamic force that shaped trade, labor, taxation, and social interactions. Its liquidity, accessibility, and cultural significance transformed it into a currency of connection, bridging gaps between individuals and city-states.

As we progress through this journey into the history of beer, we will continue to unravel the intricate roles it played in Mesopotamian society, and how its influence echoed through the ages, contributing to the evolution of beer as we know it today.

Chapter 2: Egypt: The Nectar of the Pharaohs
Ancient Egyptian Brewing Methods

In the land of the Nile, where the Pharaohs reigned and the pyramids pierced the sky, beer held a special place in the hearts and lives of the ancient Egyptians. Brewed with meticulous care and infused with reverence, Egyptian beer was more than just a drink; it was a symbol of divine providence and a testament to their mastery of brewing techniques. In this section, we delve into the fascinating world of ancient Egyptian brewing methods.

The Ingredients of Egypt

The brewing process in ancient Egypt was rooted in the use of local ingredients that reflected the agricultural bounty of the Nile Delta. While some of these ingredients were similar to those used in Mesopotamia, the unique Egyptian terroir imparted distinct flavors to their beer.

Barley: Barley was the primary grain used in Egyptian beer production, as it thrived in the fertile soil of the Nile Delta. Barley was an essential crop in Egypt, and its significance extended beyond brewing to include bread production and animal feed.

Emmer Wheat: Similar to the Sumerians, the ancient Egyptians used emmer wheat in their brewing process. This malted wheat played a crucial role in providing the necessary enzymes for fermentation.

Nile Water: The quality of water from the Nile River was vital for brewing. The consistent flow of freshwater ensured a stable supply for brewing, and the minerals in the Nile water contributed to the unique flavor profile of Egyptian beer.

Flavorings: To impart distinctive flavors to their brews, the Egyptians employed a variety of flavorings, including dates, herbs, and spices. These additions not only enhanced the taste but also extended the shelf life of the beer.

The Brewing Process

The brewing process in ancient Egypt was a blend of art and science, with strict adherence to traditions passed down through generations. While some elements were shared with Mesopotamia, the Egyptians brought their unique touch to the craft.

Malting: As in Mesopotamia, malting was a critical step in brewing. Barley or emmer wheat was soaked, allowed to sprout, and then dried. This process activated enzymes necessary for converting starches into sugars during mashing.

Milling: The malted grain was ground into coarse flour, which was then mixed with water to create a thick, dough-like mixture known as "bousa." This mixture served as the foundation for the brewing process.

Fermentation: Fermentation was a crucial phase of brewing, and the Egyptians had a deep understanding of the process. The bousa mixture was left to ferment in large, open containers. The precise temperature and duration of fermentation were closely monitored to achieve the desired flavor and alcohol content.

Straining: After fermentation, the beer was strained to remove solid particles, resulting in a clear liquid. Strainers made of reeds or similar materials were used for this purpose.

Unique Techniques: Bread and Beer

One of the distinctive features of ancient Egyptian brewing was the integration of bread into the process. Bread and beer were deeply interconnected in Egyptian culture, and their simultaneous production was a common practice.

Bread Mash: In some brewing methods, a bread mash was prepared separately and then combined with the malted grain mixture. This combination added complexity to the flavors and nutritional value of the beer.

Double Fermentation: The use of bread in brewing also led to a double fermentation process. The initial fermentation occurred during the brewing of the bread mash, and a second fermentation took place when the bread mash was combined with the malted grain mixture.

The Divine Brew

Egyptian beer was more than a culinary delight; it was an essential offering to the gods and a symbol of divine providence. Brewed with care and reverence, it played a central role in religious rituals and offerings.

Offerings to the Gods: Beer was a common offering to various Egyptian deities, including Osiris, Hathor, and Bes. Temples often brewed their own beer for religious ceremonies.

Hathor, the Goddess of Beer: Hathor, in particular, was revered as the goddess of beer and was believed to oversee the brewing process. Her blessings were sought to ensure successful fermentation.

Conclusion: The Art and Science of Egyptian Brewing

The brewing methods of ancient Egypt were a testament to the synergy of art and science. They blended local ingredients, meticulous craftsmanship, and spiritual significance to create a beverage that transcended mere sustenance. Egyptian beer was a window into their civilization, reflecting their connection to the land, their reverence for the divine, and their mastery of brewing techniques.

As we journey further into the world of ancient Egyptian beer, we will explore its symbolism in mythology, its role in daily life and rituals, and the innovations that shaped its evolution over millennia. The story of Egyptian beer is one of enduring tradition and innovation, a nectar of the Pharaohs that continues to intrigue and delight.

The Symbolism of Beer in Egyptian Mythology

In the land where the Nile River flowed like the lifeblood of the earth and the Pharaohs reigned as earthly gods, beer held a sacred place in the tapestry of Egyptian mythology. It was more than just a libation; it was a symbol of creation, sustenance, and the divine. In this section, we delve into the rich symbolism of beer in the mythology of ancient Egypt.

Hathor: Goddess of Beer and Joy

At the heart of Egyptian beer mythology stood Hathor, the goddess of beer and joy. Hathor was a multifaceted deity, associated not only with brewing but also with music, dance, love, and motherhood. Her influence on Egyptian culture was profound, and she played a central role in the symbolism of beer.

The Brewing Goddess: Hathor was often depicted as a celestial cow, symbolizing her nurturing and maternal aspects. This imagery extended to brewing, where she was seen as the divine brewer, ensuring the success of every batch of beer.

Hathor's Blessings: Brewers and consumers of beer invoked Hathor's blessings to ensure the quality and purity of their brews. She was believed to watch over the fermentation process, protecting it from spoilage and ensuring a successful outcome.

Beer as a Gift from Hathor: Beer was seen as a gift from Hathor to humanity, a manifestation of her divine grace. It was believed that her touch transformed the raw ingredients into a life-giving elixir.

Beer as the Nectar of the Gods

In Egyptian mythology, the gods themselves were known to partake in beer, elevating it to a status beyond mere sustenance. Beer was the nectar of the gods, and it played a role in the creation myth of Egypt.

Creation of Humankind: In one Egyptian creation myth, the god Ra became intoxicated on beer and subsequently vomited up the goddess Hathor. Hathor, in turn, danced and celebrated, leading to the creation of humankind. This myth emphasized beer's role in both the divine and human realms.

Beer in Divine Festivities: Beer featured prominently in the celebrations and festivals dedicated to various gods. Temples brewed their own beer for these occasions, and it was consumed as part of offerings and rituals.

Beer in the Afterlife

Egyptians believed in the afterlife and the need to prepare for the journey beyond. Beer played a crucial role in these preparations, symbolizing continuity and rejuvenation.

Funerary Offerings: Beer was included in the funerary offerings for the deceased, ensuring that they had sustenance and refreshment for the journey to the afterlife. These offerings were intended to nourish the spirits and facilitate their transition.

Resurrection and Rebirth: Beer was also associated with the concept of resurrection and rebirth. Just as the ingredients of beer were transformed through fermentation, so too were the deceased expected to undergo a transformation in the afterlife, emerging renewed and rejuvenated.

Beer in Daily Life and Rituals

While the mythology surrounding beer was deeply symbolic, its practical role in daily life and rituals was equally significant.

Daily Consumption: Beer was a staple of the Egyptian diet, enjoyed by people from all walks of life. It was consumed not only for sustenance but also as a form of hydration in the arid Egyptian climate.

Ritual Use: Beer was used in various rituals, including those related to fertility, healing, and protection. It was believed to have magical properties, and its consumption was a means of invoking divine favor.

Conclusion: The Divine Elixir

In the mythology of ancient Egypt, beer transcended its status as a mere beverage. It was a gift from the gods, a symbol of creation and rebirth, and a means of connecting with the divine. Beer was not only a reflection of Egyptian culture but also a tangible link to the spiritual realm.

As we continue our exploration of Egyptian beer in the following sections, we will uncover its role in daily life and rituals, its significance in brewing innovations, and its enduring legacy in the annals of history. The symbolism of beer in Egyptian mythology serves as a testament to the profound impact this beverage had on the civilization of the Nile.

Beer in Daily Life and Rituals

In the sun-drenched land of the Nile, where the ancient Egyptians flourished, beer was more than a beverage; it was a fundamental part of daily life and an integral component of rituals that spanned from birth to death. As we journey deeper into the heart of Egypt, we uncover the multifaceted role of beer in the lives of its people.

Sustenance and Hydration

The arid climate of Egypt made hydration a constant concern. Beer, with its nourishing properties and lower alcohol content compared to other alcoholic beverages, served as a vital source of hydration.

Everyday Beverage: Beer was an everyday drink for Egyptians of all social classes. It was consumed in homes, taverns, and workplaces, offering refreshment to laborers in the fields and sustenance to families.

Hydration in the Desert: In the harsh desert conditions outside the fertile Nile Delta, beer was a lifeline. It quenched thirst and provided essential calories, helping people endure the scorching heat.

Children and Beer: Beer's significance extended to children, who were often given diluted beer to ensure they received proper nourishment in their formative years. This practice was a testament to the nutritious value attributed to beer.

The Communal Aspect

Beer was not merely a personal beverage but a communal one, fostering bonds among family members, friends, and strangers alike.

Tavern Culture: Taverns and gathering places were central to Egyptian social life. These establishments provided a venue for people to come together, share stories, and enjoy beer.

Guest-Friendship: Sharing a drink of beer was a ritual that sealed guest-friendship, an important social custom in Egypt. Strangers would become friends through the exchange of beer, a practice that transcended social boundaries.

Community Brews: Beer was often brewed and consumed as a communal activity. Neighbors, friends, and family members would gather to assist with the brewing process, reinforcing the sense of community.

Rituals and Celebrations

Beer played a prominent role in Egyptian rituals and celebrations, marking significant life events and ensuring the favor of the gods.

Birth and Childhood: Beer was involved in birth ceremonies and the celebration of a child's arrival. It was a symbol of hope and growth for the newborn.

Marriage: Beer was a key element of marriage ceremonies and feasts. It was offered to the gods as part of the wedding rituals and shared among guests to celebrate the union.

Festivals and Religious Observances: Beer was central to various festivals dedicated to deities like Hathor and Osiris. It was offered as a libation to the gods and consumed in joyful celebrations.

Healing Rituals: Beer was also believed to have healing properties. It was used in medicinal rituals and remedies, symbolizing purification and rejuvenation.

The Transition to the Afterlife

In Egyptian culture, preparations for the afterlife were meticulous and deeply symbolic. Beer played a role in ensuring the deceased's well-being in the hereafter.

Funerary Offerings: Beer was included in the offerings to the deceased. It was believed that the spirit of the deceased would partake in these offerings, ensuring their sustenance on the journey to the afterlife.

Resurrection Symbolism: Beer was a symbol of resurrection and rebirth, paralleling the idea of the deceased's transformation in the afterlife. It represented continuity and rejuvenation.

Conclusion: Beer as a Cultural Thread

In ancient Egypt, beer was more than just a drink; it was a cultural thread that wove through the fabric of daily life, rituals, and celebrations. It quenched thirst, nourished the body, forged bonds, and connected the living with the divine and the deceased.

As we continue our exploration of Egyptian beer in the chapters ahead, we will uncover the innovations in brewing methods, the economic significance of beer, and its enduring legacy in history. The role of beer in daily life and rituals serves as a testament to its profound impact on the lives and culture of the people along the Nile.

Brewing Innovations in Ancient Egypt

In the realm of the Nile, where the desert met the fertile delta, ancient Egyptians not only mastered the art of brewing beer but also introduced innovative techniques that elevated their brews to new heights. As we delve into the world of Egyptian beer, we discover the brewing innovations that set them apart and contributed to the rich history of this iconic beverage.

The Influence of Environment

Egypt's unique geographical and climatic conditions influenced its brewing methods. The Nile River, fertile soil, and desert heat all played a role in shaping the brewing innovations of the time.

Nile Water and Barley: The Nile River provided a consistent source of freshwater, essential for both agriculture and brewing. Barley, the primary grain used in Egyptian beer, thrived in the fertile soil nourished by the river's annual flooding.

Natural Fermentation: The warm climate of Egypt accelerated the fermentation process. Compared to Mesopotamia, where brewers relied on wild yeast, Egyptian brewers had the advantage of a more predictable and rapid fermentation due to higher temperatures.

Bread and Beer: A Symbiotic Relationship

One of the most distinctive features of Egyptian brewing was the integration of bread into the process. Bread and beer were intertwined, and this symbiotic relationship led to unique innovations.

Bread Mash: In Egyptian brewing, a bread mash was often prepared separately. This bread mash was made from a mixture of emmer wheat and water, creating a dough-like substance known as "bousa." The bousa was then fermented, and the resulting liquid was added to the primary beer mixture.

Double Fermentation: The use of a bread mash introduced a double fermentation process. The initial fermentation occurred during the preparation of the bread mash, and a second fermentation took place when the bread mash was combined with the malted grain mixture. This complex process contributed to the flavor profile and nutritional value of Egyptian beer.

Clay Vessels and Storage

The choice of materials and techniques for brewing and storing beer in Egypt was distinct and influenced the final product.

Clay Fermentation Vessels: Egyptian brewers used clay pots or amphorae for fermentation. These vessels were not only readily available but also provided a stable and cool environment for fermentation. The porous nature of clay allowed for some degree of aeration, contributing to the flavor profile of the beer.

Sealing and Preservation: To prevent contamination and oxidation, brewers sealed the clay vessels with lids made of mud or clay. This sealing technique helped preserve the beer and maintain its quality over time.

Beer Quality and Consistency

Egyptian brewers placed a strong emphasis on the quality and consistency of their beer, developing methods to ensure a reliable product.

Sensory Evaluation: Brewers relied on sensory evaluation to assess the quality of their beer. They used their senses of taste, smell, and sight to detect any off-flavors or spoilage.

Recipes and Standardization: Brewing methods were documented, and recipes were passed down through generations. This standardization ensured that each batch of beer met specific quality criteria.

Religious Oversight: In many cases, temples oversaw beer production. This religious oversight not only ensured the purity of the beer but also upheld the sanctity of the brewing process.

The Legacy of Egyptian Brewing

The innovations in brewing techniques and the symbiotic relationship between bread and beer in ancient Egypt left a lasting legacy. While some of these techniques may seem archaic by modern standards, they contributed to the rich history of brewing and set the stage for future developments in the world of beer.

As we continue our exploration of Egyptian beer in the chapters ahead, we will uncover its significance in trade and economy, its role in daily life and rituals, and its enduring influence on the broader history of beer. The innovations in brewing methods serve as a testament to the ingenuity of the ancient Egyptians and their deep connection to this beloved elixir.

Chapter 3: Ancient Europe: Monasteries and Medieval Brews

Monastic Brewing Traditions

In the heart of medieval Europe, amid the solemn cloisters and devout prayers of monasteries, a brewing tradition of unparalleled significance emerged. Monastic brewing was more than a craft; it was a sacred duty, a source of sustenance, and a legacy that would shape the history of beer. As we explore the world of monastic brewing traditions, we uncover the spiritual devotion, innovation, and enduring impact that characterized this remarkable chapter in the history of beer.

The Monastic Way of Life

To understand monastic brewing, one must first appreciate the monastic way of life. Monasteries were havens of solitude and spirituality, where monks devoted their lives to prayer, contemplation, and the pursuit of God's work on Earth. Yet, within this austere existence, brewing found its place as both a practical necessity and a divine calling.

Self-Sufficiency: Monasteries were often self-sufficient, and brewing was one of the essential crafts practiced within their walls. Monks brewed beer not only for their own sustenance but also as a means of supporting the monastery and its charitable works.

Ora et Labora: The Benedictine motto "Ora et Labora," which translates to "Pray and Work," encapsulated the monastic philosophy. Brewing became a form of labor through which monks could glorify God and serve their communities.

Benedictine Influence: The Benedictine Order played a pivotal role in the development of monastic brewing. St. Benedict himself included brewing as part of the daily routine outlined in his Rule, which became the guiding principle for many monastic communities.

The Spiritual Significance

For monks, brewing was a spiritual journey, and every aspect of the process held profound meaning.

Sacramental Connection: Monastic brewing was deeply rooted in the idea of transubstantiation—the transformation of bread and wine into the body and blood of Christ during the Eucharist. Beer, as a product of grain, water, and yeast, was seen as a reflection of this sacred process.

God's Work: Brewing was regarded as "God's work" or "the work of God's hands." Monks saw their labor as a form of prayer, and they approached each step of the brewing process with reverence and devotion.

Divine Blessing: Monastic breweries often featured chapels or altars, and brewing sessions began with prayers for God's blessing on the process. The belief was that God's favor was necessary for the success of the brew.

Brewing Innovations

Monastic brewing traditions also introduced several innovations that would later influence the broader beer world.

Quality and Consistency: Monks were meticulous in their approach to brewing, emphasizing quality and consistency. They kept detailed records, refined brewing techniques, and developed standardized recipes.

Hops and Flavoring: Monks are often credited with introducing hops as a flavoring and preservative agent in beer. This innovation not only enhanced the flavor but also extended the shelf life of their brews.

Abbey Beers: Monastic breweries often produced unique styles of beer, known as "abbey beers." These brews were distinct to each monastery and served as a source of income and reputation.

The Trappist Tradition

The Trappist tradition represents a subset of monastic brewing that adheres to strict guidelines and produces some of the most highly regarded beers in the world.

Trappist Values: Trappist breweries operate under the guiding principles of the International Trappist Association. They prioritize self-sufficiency, quality, and social responsibility.

The Trappist Six: As of the present day, there are six Trappist breweries in Belgium—Orval, Chimay, Rochefort, Westmalle, Westvleteren, and Achel—each producing its unique range of abbey beers.

Conclusion: A Spiritual Brew

Monastic brewing traditions are a testament to the intersection of faith, craft, and innovation. For monks, brewing was a divine calling, a means of sustenance, and a legacy that transcended generations. The reverence and dedication with which they approached their craft continue to inspire brewers and beer enthusiasts around the world.

As we journey further into the world of monastic brewing in the following chapters, we will explore the influence of monasteries on medieval European beer production, their role in shaping modern beer styles, and their enduring legacy in the modern craft beer revival. The monastic brewing traditions stand as a testament to the enduring spirit of innovation and devotion that has characterized the world of beer for centuries.

The Monks' Contribution to Beer Production

In the quiet solitude of medieval European monasteries, monks undertook a sacred mission that would leave an indelible mark on the history of beer. Their devotion to prayer was matched only by their dedication to brewing, and the contributions of these monks to beer production went far beyond the walls of their cloisters. As we explore the world of monastic brewing, we uncover the monks' invaluable contributions to the craft, from innovation in brewing techniques to their role as pioneers in beer production.

Preserving the Brewing Tradition

As the Roman Empire crumbled and the Dark Ages descended upon Europe, much of the knowledge and techniques of brewing faced the risk of being lost to history. It was the monks who stepped forward to preserve this ancient craft.

Monastic Libraries: Monasteries were repositories of knowledge in a time when few institutions dedicated themselves to learning. Monks meticulously copied and safeguarded brewing manuscripts and texts, ensuring the preservation of brewing traditions.

Innovation and Experimentation: Within the confines of their monasteries, monks continued to innovate and experiment with brewing techniques. They refined existing methods and developed new recipes, pushing the boundaries of what was known.

Quality and Consistency

One of the defining contributions of monks to brewing was their unwavering commitment to quality and consistency. This devotion to excellence would set a standard for the brewing industry that endures to this day.

Records and Documentation: Monastic breweries kept meticulous records of their brewing processes. They recorded ingredients, measurements, and procedures to achieve a consistent product.

Standardized Recipes: The monks developed standardized recipes for their beers. This consistency was vital, as their brews were often distributed to surrounding communities and were a source of income for the monastery.

Hops as a Flavoring Agent: Monks are often credited with introducing hops as a flavoring and preservative agent in beer. This innovation not only enhanced the flavor but also extended the shelf life of their brews.

The Role of Monasteries

Monasteries played a central role in the brewing landscape of medieval Europe, and their impact on the development of beer production was profound.

Monastic Economies: Monasteries were often self-sufficient communities. Brewing beer was not only a source of sustenance for the monks but also a means of generating income to support their charitable works and maintain the monastery.

Local Economies: The presence of monasteries had a significant influence on the local economies. They were centers of trade and commerce, and their beers became sought-after commodities, contributing to the economic development of surrounding regions.

Monastic Breweries: Monasteries were home to some of the most advanced breweries of their time. They featured state-of-the-art equipment and facilities that set them apart as brewing centers.

The Trappist Tradition

Within the world of monastic brewing, the Trappist tradition stands as a pinnacle of dedication to the craft and spiritual values.

International Trappist Association: The International Trappist Association sets stringent criteria for what qualifies as a Trappist brewery. These criteria ensure that Trappist beers are brewed within the walls of a Trappist monastery and adhere to principles of quality, self-sufficiency, and social responsibility.

Trappist Breweries: As of the present day, there are several Trappist breweries in Europe and beyond, each producing a range of renowned abbey beers. The Trappist tradition continues to be a standard-bearer for excellence in brewing.

A Legacy That Endures

The monks' contribution to beer production was not limited to their time but left an enduring legacy that continues to influence the brewing industry today. Their devotion to quality, consistency, and innovation paved the way for the diverse world of beer that we know today.

As we journey further into the world of monastic brewing in the following chapters, we will explore the significance of beer in medieval European society, the influence of monasteries on modern beer styles, and the enduring impact of the monks' dedication to the craft. The monks' contribution to beer production is a testament to the enduring spirit of craftsmanship and devotion that has shaped the history of beer for centuries.

Beer in Medieval Europe

In the heart of medieval Europe, beer flowed as a vital elixir, sustaining the daily lives of peasants, nobility, and clergy alike. As we journey back in time to the Middle Ages, we discover the central role that beer played in the social, cultural, and economic tapestry of medieval European society.

A Necessity of Life

Beer was not a mere luxury; it was a fundamental necessity of life in medieval Europe. The conditions and challenges of the time made beer a ubiquitous and indispensable companion for people of all walks of life.

Sanitation and Safety: The water supply in medieval towns and villages was often contaminated and unsafe to drink. Beer, with its alcohol content, provided a safe alternative, free from waterborne diseases.

Nutrition and Calories: For peasants and laborers, beer was a valuable source of nutrition and calories. It provided essential sustenance, especially during periods of scarcity.

Diversity of Brews: Medieval Europe saw a wide variety of beer styles, ranging from mild table beers to stronger ales and meads. These brews catered to different tastes and nutritional needs.

Beer as a Staple Food

In some regions, beer was not just a beverage; it was considered a staple food, akin to bread. It formed a significant part of the daily diet for many Europeans.

Bread and Beer: In some areas, beer was referred to as "liquid bread." It provided calories, protein, and essential nutrients, particularly during harsh winters or lean times.

Beer Soup: In certain culinary traditions, beer was used to prepare hearty soups and stews. These dishes combined beer with grains, vegetables, and sometimes meat, creating filling and nutritious meals.

Monastic Influence: Monasteries, with their expertise in brewing, often produced beers that were not only consumed as beverages but also used as food in their communal meals.

Brewing Guilds and Regulations

Medieval European cities and towns often had brewing guilds that regulated the brewing industry. These guilds played a crucial role in ensuring the quality and safety of beer.

Brewing Guilds: Brewing guilds were associations of brewers that established standards for brewing and trade. They maintained quality control and protected the interests of their members.

Brewing Regulations: Cities and towns often imposed strict regulations on brewing, covering everything from ingredient quality to the pricing of beer. These regulations helped maintain order in the brewing industry.

Quality Control: Brews were often subject to tasting panels or inspections to ensure that they met established standards. Poor-quality beer could result in fines or expulsion from the guild.

Beer and Religion

Religion and beer were closely intertwined in medieval Europe. The church played a significant role in the production and distribution of beer.

Monastic Brewing: Monasteries were prolific brewers, and their beers were not only used in religious ceremonies but also distributed to local communities and sold to fund charitable works.

Beer as a Tithe: In some regions, beer was offered as a tithe to the church. Parishioners would provide a portion of their beer production as an offering to support the clergy and maintain the church.

Fasting and Beer: During fasting periods, when meat and rich foods were restricted, beer was often allowed as a source of sustenance. It was considered a liquid form of nourishment.

Social and Cultural Significance

Beer was a social lubricant and a symbol of celebration in medieval Europe. It played a vital role in gatherings, festivals, and communal life.

Taverns and Social Hubs: Taverns were central gathering places in medieval towns. They offered beer and provided a space for socializing, storytelling, and community bonding.

Festivals and Celebrations: Beer was integral to medieval festivals and celebrations. It was often served in abundance during weddings, fairs, and religious holidays, fostering a sense of unity and merriment.

Songs and Stories: Beer-inspired songs and stories were a part of medieval culture. Bards and minstrels celebrated the virtues of beer, and tales of alewives and brewers were passed down through generations.

Conclusion: A Brew of History

In the tapestry of medieval European life, beer stood as a common thread that connected people across social strata. It was more than just a beverage; it was sustenance, tradition, and a symbol of unity. As we continue our journey through the annals of beer history, we will explore its enduring influence on modern brewing, its role in shaping European identity, and the innovations that would pave the way for the craft beer revolution. The story of beer in medieval Europe is a brew of history, culture, and tradition that continues to flow through the ages.

The Influence of Monasteries on Modern Brewing

The legacy of medieval European monasteries extends far beyond their sacred walls. Their contributions to the art and science of brewing have left an indelible mark on the modern beer landscape. As we explore the enduring influence of monasteries on contemporary brewing practices, we uncover the threads of tradition, innovation, and craftsmanship that continue to shape the world of beer today.

Preservation of Brewing Knowledge

One of the most significant contributions of monasteries to modern brewing is the preservation of brewing knowledge during times of upheaval and change.

Manuscript Copying: Monasteries served as repositories of knowledge, meticulously copying and preserving brewing manuscripts, texts, and recipes. Many of these documents have survived to the present day, providing valuable insights into historical brewing practices.

Transcription and Translation: Monks often translated brewing texts from Latin and other languages, making this knowledge accessible to a broader audience. This dissemination of brewing knowledge laid the foundation for future generations of brewers.

Quality and Consistency

The emphasis on quality and consistency in monastic brewing has become a cornerstone of modern brewing practices.

Record-Keeping: Monasteries maintained detailed records of their brewing processes, ingredients, and outcomes. This commitment to documentation laid the groundwork for quality control and repeatability in modern brewing.

Standardization: Monks developed standardized recipes for their brews, ensuring that each batch met specific quality criteria. This approach to consistency is echoed in modern brewing where adherence to recipes and processes is paramount.

Hops as a Flavoring Agent: Monks' use of hops as a flavoring and preservative agent revolutionized brewing. This innovation not only enhanced the flavor of their brews but also contributed to the development of modern beer styles.

Trappist Breweries

The Trappist tradition, rooted in monastic values of self-sufficiency and quality, continues to thrive and influence modern brewing.

Strict Criteria: Trappist breweries must adhere to strict criteria set by the International Trappist Association.

These criteria ensure that Trappist beers are brewed within the walls of a Trappist monastery and uphold principles of quality, social responsibility, and self-sufficiency.

Global Presence: Trappist breweries can be found not only in Europe but also in other parts of the world. Each Trappist brewery produces a unique range of highly regarded abbey beers, continuing the tradition of excellence and devotion.

Inspiring Craft Brewers: The dedication of Trappist breweries to their craft and values has inspired countless craft brewers worldwide to prioritize quality, tradition, and community involvement.

Beer Styles and Techniques

Monasteries played a pivotal role in the development of beer styles and brewing techniques that are still celebrated today.

Belgian Abbey Ales: The brewing traditions of Belgian abbeys, including Trappist monasteries, have given rise to iconic beer styles such as Dubbel, Tripel, and Quadrupel. These styles are cherished by beer enthusiasts worldwide.

Strong Ales and Barleywines: The strong ales brewed by monks, often for special occasions and holidays, laid the foundation for modern barleywines and strong ale styles.

Monastic Techniques: Monastic breweries employed techniques such as bottle conditioning and wild yeast fermentation, which continue to influence modern craft brewing. These methods are celebrated for their contribution to flavor complexity.

Conclusion: A Timeless Brew

The influence of monasteries on modern brewing is a testament to the enduring spirit of craftsmanship, tradition, and innovation. From the preservation of knowledge to the dedication to quality, monastic brewing values continue to shape the beer industry. As we delve further into the world of beer, we will explore the revival of historical brewing techniques, the diversity of contemporary beer styles, and the enduring appeal of craftsmanship and community in the modern craft beer movement. The timeless brew of monastic influence continues to flow through the ages, enriching the world of beer with its enduring legacy.

Chapter 4: Ancient Asia: Beyond the Cradle of Civilization

Chinese and Indian Brewing Traditions

As we venture beyond the cradle of civilization, into the vast and diverse landscapes of ancient Asia, we encounter brewing traditions that have thrived for millennia. Chinese and Indian brewing traditions are steeped in history, culture, and innovation, offering unique insights into the art of brewing and the profound impact of beer on these ancient civilizations.

Chinese Brewing Traditions

Ancient Origins: Brewing in China dates back over 5,000 years. Archaeological evidence reveals the use of millet, barley, and rice in early Chinese brewing. These ancient brews were integral to rituals and celebrations.

Rice Wine and Beer: Chinese brewing traditions encompass a wide range of alcoholic beverages, including rice wines like "jiu" and beer-like beverages made from grains. These brews were enjoyed in both everyday life and religious ceremonies.

Fermentation Jars: Ancient Chinese brewers used distinctive pottery jars for fermentation. These jars played a crucial role in the fermentation process and are a testament to the craftsmanship of the time.

Chinese Brewing Techniques

Fermentation: In China, fermentation was a central aspect of brewing. The process was often natural, relying on wild yeast and ambient microorganisms. These spontaneous fermentations contributed to the unique flavor profiles of Chinese brews.

Medicinal Brews: Chinese brewing was closely tied to traditional medicine. Many brews were believed to have medicinal properties and were used to address various health concerns.

Rituals and Ancestral Worship: Chinese brewing played a pivotal role in rituals and ancestral worship. Offerings of alcoholic beverages were made to ancestors, deities, and spirits as a form of reverence and communication.

Indian Brewing Traditions

Ancient India: Brewing in ancient India was diverse and deeply rooted in cultural and religious practices. Various grains, such as barley, rice, and millet, were used to create a wide array of alcoholic beverages.

Soma Ritual: The Rigveda, one of the oldest sacred texts of Hinduism, mentions the "soma" ritual, which involved the consumption of a sacred drink believed to grant divine insights and immortality. While the exact nature of soma remains a subject of debate, it is thought to have been a fermented beverage.

Arrack and Toddy: In addition to grain-based brews, India was known for the production of "arrack" and "toddy." Arrack, a distilled spirit, was produced from the sap of various palm trees. Toddy was the sweet sap collected from palm trees, often fermented to create a mildly alcoholic beverage.

Influence of Spices and Herbs

Both Chinese and Indian brewing traditions incorporated an array of spices, herbs, and botanicals to enhance flavor and aroma.

Chinese Spices: Chinese brews often featured spices such as ginger, cinnamon, and star anise. These additions not only added complexity to the flavors but also held cultural significance.

Indian Spices: Indian brews were known for the use of spices like cardamom, black pepper, and cloves. These spices contributed to the aromatic and flavorful profiles of Indian brews.

Ayurveda: In India, the use of herbs and spices in brewing was closely connected to Ayurveda, the traditional system of medicine. Brews were often imbued with medicinal herbs for their healing properties.

Legacy and Revival

While ancient Chinese and Indian brewing traditions faced challenges and declines over the centuries, there has been a recent resurgence of interest in these historical practices.

Craft Brewers: Contemporary craft brewers in China and India are reviving traditional brewing techniques and ingredients. They are producing unique and innovative brews that pay homage to their cultural heritage.

Cultural Heritage: The preservation and celebration of brewing traditions as cultural heritage have gained recognition. Efforts are underway to document and protect these ancient practices for future generations.

Global Influence: Chinese and Indian flavors and ingredients have made their mark on the global brewing scene. Craft breweries around the world are experimenting with spices, herbs, and grains inspired by these traditions.

Conclusion: Ancient Brews, Modern Resurgence

The brewing traditions of ancient China and India offer a glimpse into the rich tapestry of Asian cultures and the enduring appeal of beer throughout history. As we continue our exploration of brewing in Asia, we will delve into the cultural significance of beer, its role in trade along the Silk Road, and the diverse array of beverages that have flowed from the ancient to the modern world. The legacy of Chinese and Indian brewing traditions is a testament to the timelessness of beer as a cultural, culinary, and social phenomenon.

Rice, Millet, and Sorghum Brews

In the vast landscapes of ancient Asia, where rice paddies, millet fields, and sorghum crops thrived, brewing took on a diverse and vibrant character. The use of these grains for brewing purposes produced a wide array of unique and flavorful brews, each deeply rooted in the cultural and agricultural traditions of their respective regions.

Rice: The Elixir of the East

Rice Brewing Origins: Rice brewing has a rich history that stretches back thousands of years, primarily in East and Southeast Asia. This grain was not only a staple food but also a source of inspiration for brewers.

Sake in Japan: Sake, Japan's iconic rice wine, holds a special place in Japanese culture. Its production involves a meticulous process of rice milling, steaming, fermentation, and meticulous craftsmanship.

Soju in Korea: Korea is known for its own rice-based spirit, soju. Originally derived from sake, it evolved into a distinctive Korean alcoholic beverage with various flavor profiles and strengths.

China's Rice Wines: In China, rice wine traditions vary by region, producing a multitude of rice-based alcoholic beverages. These brews can range from sweet to dry, still to sparkling, and low-alcohol to high-proof.

Millet: The Grain of Many Names

Ancient Millet Use: Millet was one of the earliest domesticated grains in Asia and played a significant role in brewing practices across different regions.

Baijiu in China: China's baijiu, a strong distilled spirit, is traditionally made from sorghum, wheat, or rice, but millet has also been used. Its unique flavor profiles and production methods have made it a cultural treasure.

Kodo in India: In India, the use of millet in brewing can be traced back to ancient times. "Kodo" and "kutki" are fermented millet-based beverages that are enjoyed in various parts of the country.

Millet Brews in Africa: Beyond Asia, millet has been used for brewing in Africa for centuries. Sorghum and millet beers are staples in many African cultures and are celebrated for their unique flavors and cultural significance.

Sorghum: A Diverse Grain

Sorghum Brewing Traditions: Sorghum, a drought-resistant grain, has been a valuable resource for brewing in regions with arid climates.

African Sorghum Beers: In Africa, sorghum-based beers such as "tella," "merisa," and "dolo" are cherished for their role in daily life, rituals, and celebrations. These brews offer a fascinating glimpse into the intersection of agriculture and brewing.

Sorghum and Maize in the Americas: In the Americas, indigenous cultures like the Aztecs and Mayans brewed fermented beverages using sorghum and maize (corn), creating traditions that persist in modern Mexican and Central American cultures.

Sorghum Beer Revival: Today, there is a growing interest in sorghum-based beers in the craft brewing scene. These brews cater to those with gluten sensitivities and contribute to the diversity of beer styles.

Brewing Techniques and Fermentation

Sake Fermentation: Sake brewing involves a unique fermentation process that uses a special mold called "koji" to convert rice starches into fermentable sugars. The use of multiple parallel fermentations contributes to sake's complexity.

Sorghum Fermentation: Sorghum-based brews, whether in Africa or the Americas, often involve natural fermentation with wild yeast and lactic acid bacteria. These fermentations result in a wide range of flavor profiles and characteristics.

Rice Brewing Innovations: Modern sake production has seen innovations, including the use of modern equipment and techniques while preserving traditional craftsmanship. The "junmai" movement emphasizes purity and simplicity in sake production.

Conclusion: Grains of Tradition

The use of rice, millet, and sorghum in brewing traditions across Asia and beyond reflects the deep connection between agriculture, culture, and the art of fermentation. As we continue our exploration of ancient Asian brewing, we will delve into the cultural significance of these brews, their role along the Silk Road, and the enduring appeal of grain-based fermentations. The grains of tradition continue to be a source of inspiration for brewers, offering a diverse palette of flavors and traditions that enrich the world of beer and spirits.

The Cultural Significance of Beer in Asia

Beer has long held a place of honor in the diverse cultures of Asia. Its production and consumption have been woven into the fabric of daily life, rituals, and celebrations across the continent. In this exploration of the cultural significance of beer in Asia, we discover the deep-rooted traditions, social connections, and spiritual meanings that have made beer an integral part of Asian heritage.

Rituals and Ceremonies

Offerings to Ancestors: In many Asian cultures, beer has played a central role in ancestral worship. It is offered to honor and appease the spirits of ancestors, ensuring their continued protection and goodwill.

Birth and Weddings: Beer is often present during life's milestones. It is served to celebrate births, marriages, and other significant events. Beer's presence signifies blessings and good fortune.

Religious Festivals: Beer is frequently used in religious ceremonies and festivals. It serves as a symbol of purification, spiritual communion, and the divine presence.

Social Bonding

Community and Communion: Beer is a universal social lubricant that brings people together. It fosters a sense of community and kinship, whether in small villages or bustling cities.

Taverns and Teahouses: In many Asian societies, taverns, teahouses, and similar establishments serve as social hubs. They are places where people gather to unwind, share stories, and form lasting connections over a glass of beer.

Business and Networking: Beer has played a role in business and networking for centuries. Business deals and negotiations are often sealed over a drink, strengthening partnerships and trust.

Regional Variations

Baijiu in China: China's baijiu, a strong distilled spirit, is deeply ingrained in Chinese culture. It is used in toasts, business banquets, and formal gatherings, symbolizing hospitality and goodwill.

Sake in Japan: Sake holds a revered position in Japanese culture. The Japanese language even has specific terms and etiquette for sake consumption. Sake breweries often host ceremonies and festivals celebrating their craft.

Rice Beers in Southeast Asia: Southeast Asian countries like Thailand and Vietnam have their own versions of rice-based beers. These brews are enjoyed during local festivals and ceremonies, reflecting the tropical climates and agricultural traditions of the region.

Beer and Cuisine

Pairing with Food: Beer's versatility makes it an ideal accompaniment to a wide range of Asian cuisines. From spicy Thai curries to delicate sushi, beer complements the flavors and enhances dining experiences.

Beer and Street Food: Street food vendors across Asia often serve beer alongside their offerings. These casual pairings create a vibrant street dining culture where locals and tourists alike can savor local flavors.

Culinary Innovations: The craft beer movement in Asia has led to culinary innovations, such as beer-infused dishes and pairing menus. Beer has become a versatile ingredient for creative chefs and home cooks.

Modern Craft Beer Renaissance

Craft Beer Boom: In recent years, Asia has experienced a craft beer renaissance. Microbreweries and craft beer bars have sprung up across the continent, offering diverse and innovative brews.

Blending Tradition and Innovation: Craft brewers in Asia often draw inspiration from traditional brewing methods and local ingredients while embracing modern techniques. This fusion results in unique and culturally resonant beers.

Beer Tourism: The growth of the craft beer industry has led to beer tourism, where enthusiasts visit breweries, attend beer festivals, and explore the rich tapestry of beer culture in Asia.

Conclusion: A Toast to Tradition

The cultural significance of beer in Asia is a testament to its enduring appeal as a beverage that bridges generations, fosters connections, and symbolizes the richness of cultural heritage. As we journey further into the world of Asian brewing, we will explore the historical trade routes that connected beer-producing regions, the impact of colonialism on brewing traditions, and the diverse array of flavors and traditions that continue to thrive in the modern Asian beer scene. Beer's role in Asian cultures is not just a beverage; it's a heartfelt toast to tradition, unity, and the shared joy of life.

Beer Along the Silk Road

The Silk Road, an ancient network of trade routes that connected the East and West, served as a conduit not only for goods but also for culture, ideas, and, of course, beer. As we embark on a journey along this historic route, we'll uncover the pivotal role beer played in facilitating trade, fostering cross-cultural exchanges, and leaving an indelible mark on the societies it touched.

The Silk Road: A Historical Marvel

Origins and Significance: The Silk Road emerged during the Han Dynasty of China and thrived for centuries. It facilitated the exchange of silk, spices, precious metals, art, and ideas between the East and West.

Diversity of Cultures: The Silk Road passed through a mosaic of cultures, languages, and landscapes. It connected regions as diverse as China, India, Central Asia, the Middle East, and Europe.

Caravan Trade: Caravans of camels, horses, and traders traversed vast deserts, mountains, and plains, overcoming tremendous challenges to transport goods.

Beer as a Trade Commodity

Silk and Spices: While silk, spices, and precious metals were among the most famous commodities traded along the Silk Road, beer also played a significant role in this exchange.

Transporting Brews: Brewers and merchants transported various forms of beer, including beer bricks, which were dehydrated for easier transport, and beer in ceramic vessels.

Exchange of Knowledge: The trade of beer also facilitated the exchange of brewing techniques, ingredients, and cultures between East and West. This sharing of knowledge enriched the art of brewing in both regions.

Ancient Beer Trade Routes

From China to Europe: The Silk Road had multiple branches that crisscrossed the continent. Brews made in China, India, and Central Asia traveled westward, eventually reaching Europe.

Central Asian Oasis Towns: Oasis towns in Central Asia, such as Samarkand and Bukhara, served as crucial hubs for trade and rest. Here, traders and travelers could find respite and enjoy local brews.

Beer in the Middle East: As beer made its way westward, it became a staple in Middle Eastern cultures. It was enjoyed in palaces, taverns, and on the streets of bustling markets.

Brewing Techniques and Innovations

Yeasts and Fermentation: The exchange of yeasts along the Silk Road played a pivotal role in shaping the flavors of beer. Different yeasts contributed to diverse beer styles.

Spices and Botanicals: The Silk Road's trade routes brought an array of spices, herbs, and botanicals that enriched the flavors of beer. These ingredients continue to be used in brewing today.

Ceramic and Glass Vessels: The development and widespread use of ceramic and glass vessels for brewing and storing beer were significant innovations along the Silk Road.

Cultural Exchange

Religious Influence: Buddhism, Islam, Zoroastrianism, and other religions along the Silk Road often had specific attitudes toward alcohol. Beer, influenced by these beliefs, took on various roles in religious practices.

Art and Literature: The Silk Road fostered the exchange of art, literature, and ideas. Beer appeared in stories, paintings, and artifacts, reflecting its cultural importance.

Language and Names: The Silk Road introduced new words for beer and brewing techniques to different languages, demonstrating the depth of cultural exchange.

Legacy and Revival

Modern Craft Breweries: Today, craft breweries along the ancient Silk Road routes draw inspiration from history. They create brews that pay homage to traditional recipes and ingredients while embracing modern innovations.

Cultural Festivals: Across regions once connected by the Silk Road, beer festivals and cultural events celebrate the historical significance of beer and the enduring connections it represents.

Tourism and Heritage: Breweries and archaeological sites related to beer production along the Silk Road have become tourist attractions and heritage sites, preserving the memory of this ancient trade.

Conclusion: A Liquid Legacy

The Silk Road, a marvel of human enterprise, not only facilitated the exchange of goods but also provided a conduit for the exchange of culture, including the beloved beverage of beer. As we continue our exploration of beer's journey through Asia, we will delve into the impact of colonialism on brewing traditions, the enduring appeal of traditional beer styles, and the remarkable diversity of flavors and cultures that have flowed along this historic route. The legacy of beer along the Silk Road is a testament to its power to unite, inspire, and transcend boundaries—a liquid legacy that still enriches our world today.

Chapter 5: Nordic Nectar: Beer in Northern Europe
Viking Brewing Techniques

The Vikings, famed for their seafaring prowess and adventurous spirit, also had a deep appreciation for the art of brewing. As we journey into the heart of Northern Europe, we discover the brewing techniques and traditions that fueled the Viking age and helped define their cultural identity.

Viking Brewing: A Historical Perspective

Viking Seafaring: The Vikings, who flourished between the 8th and 11th centuries, roamed across Europe, Asia, and even North America. Their longships carried not only warriors but also the makings of their beloved brews.

Barley and Wheat: Barley and wheat were the primary grains used by the Vikings for brewing. These grains were cultivated in the region and played a central role in daily life.

Ale, Not Beer: The Vikings brewed a form of ale rather than what we consider beer today. Their brews were typically unfiltered and had a cloudy appearance.

Ingredients and Recipes

Malt Production: Malting was a crucial step in Viking brewing. Barley or wheat was soaked, allowed to germinate, and then dried. This process converted starches into fermentable sugars.

Wild Herbs and Botanicals: Vikings flavored their ale with a variety of wild herbs and botanicals, such as bog myrtle, yarrow, juniper, and heather. These additives not only contributed to flavor but also acted as preservatives.

Water Source: Access to clean water was vital for brewing, and Vikings often established settlements near reliable water sources.

Brewing Process

Mashing and Lautering: The Vikings mashed their malted grains with hot water, creating a sugary liquid known as wort. After mashing, they would lautering to separate the liquid from the solid grain material.

Boiling: The wort was boiled, and during this process, hops or other flavoring agents were added. Hops were not commonly used by Vikings, but when they were, it added bitterness and acted as a preservative.

Fermentation: Once the wort cooled, it was transferred to fermentation vessels. Vikings used open fermenters and relied on wild yeast for fermentation.

Viking Ale in Society

Social and Ceremonial: Viking ale held a central place in social gatherings and ceremonies. It was consumed during feasts, weddings, and funerals. Ale was often shared as a sign of hospitality and goodwill.

Religious Offerings: Ale was also used as an offering to Norse deities like Odin and Thor. The Vikings believed that sharing ale with the gods could bring favor and protection.

Economic Importance: Brewing was not only a cultural practice but also an economic one. Vikings traded ale with neighboring cultures and used it as a form of currency in some transactions.

Brewing Vessels and Techniques

Wooden Barrels: Vikings used wooden barrels made from oak and other woods for brewing and storage. These barrels contributed to the flavors of the ale and allowed for ease of transport.

Souring Techniques: Some Viking ales were intentionally soured through wild fermentation, resulting in complex, tart flavors similar to modern sour ales.

Brewing Tools: Viking brewers used a variety of tools, such as wooden mash paddles and horn spoons, to manage their brewing processes.

Modern Interpretations

Experimental Archaeology: Archaeologists and brewers have collaborated to recreate Viking-era ales, using historical recipes and techniques. These experiments provide insights into the flavors and brewing methods of the time.

Modern Viking Ales: Craft breweries in Northern Europe and beyond have drawn inspiration from Viking brewing traditions. They produce a range of ales that pay homage to the flavors and ingredients of the past.

Cultural Revival: In regions with strong Viking heritage, cultural festivals and events celebrate the Viking age, often featuring traditional ale brewing and tasting.

Conclusion: Raising a Horn to Tradition

The Vikings' passion for brewing and their unique techniques reflect the rich tapestry of Northern European culture during their era. As we continue our exploration of beer's history in Northern Europe, we will delve into the mythology and cultural significance of beer in Norse society, the enduring legacy of Viking ale in contemporary craft brewing, and the timeless appeal of raising a horn to tradition—a tradition that connects us with the adventurous spirit of the past.

Beer in Norse Mythology

In the heart of Northern Europe, where the rugged landscapes are shaped by glaciers, fjords, and ancient forests, beer held a special place in Norse culture and mythology. It was not just a beverage but a symbol of divine celebration, storytelling, and the deep connections between gods and mortals.

The Mythic Mead: A Cosmic Beverage

The Mead of Poetry: In Norse mythology, there exists a mythical mead called "Mead of Poetry" or "Sôma," which granted the gift of eloquence and poetic inspiration to those who consumed it.

The Cosmic Context: The creation of this mead is deeply entwined with the cosmic saga of the Aesir gods, the Vanir gods, and the Jotnar (giants). It represents the power of storytelling and the preservation of knowledge.

Kvasir's Blood: The Mead of Poetry's origins are rooted in the tale of Kvasir, a wise being created from the spittle of the Aesir and Vanir gods. His blood was used to create the mead after his tragic death.

The Mead of Poetry: A Divine Quest

Odin's Quest: In Norse mythology, the Allfather Odin coveted the Mead of Poetry. To obtain it, he embarked on a daring journey that took him to the realm of the giants, where the mead was guarded by a giantess named Gunnlod.

The Sacrifices: Odin faced numerous trials and made great sacrifices on his quest. He hung himself from the world tree, Yggdrasil, for nine days and nights, without food or water, in exchange for the mead.

The Theft of the Mead: After securing the mead, Odin returned to Asgard, the realm of the gods, where he shared the mead with select mortals, granting them the gift of poetry and wisdom.

Beer and Storytelling

Skalds and Poets: In Norse society, skilled poets and storytellers, known as skalds, played a pivotal role. They were revered for their ability to craft poems and sagas that celebrated the deeds of heroes and gods.

Hall of Bragi: The "Hall of Bragi" was a place in Asgard dedicated to poetry and storytelling. It was here that gods and mortals gathered to share mead and stories, preserving their history and culture.

Eddas and Sagas: Norse mythology and history were passed down through written texts like the Poetic Edda and the Prose Edda. These manuscripts were repositories of knowledge and inspiration.

Beer in Ritual and Celebration

Feasting and Sacrifice: Beer and mead were central to Norse feasts and celebrations. They were offered to gods and spirits as a form of sacrifice and communion.

Weddings and Alliances: Beer played a role in forging alliances and sealing marriage vows. It was consumed during weddings and celebrations of diplomatic agreements.

Funerals and Ancestral Worship: Beer was also poured as offerings to honor the deceased and ancestors, ensuring their protection and goodwill in the afterlife.

Modern Interpretations

Craft Brewers and Mythology: Contemporary craft brewers in Northern Europe draw inspiration from Norse mythology. Some create beers that pay homage to the Mead of Poetry or incorporate traditional ingredients and flavors.

Mythic Imagery: Labels and branding often feature mythic imagery from Norse tales, celebrating the rich storytelling tradition of the region.

Cultural Festivals: Cultural festivals and events in Northern Europe showcase Norse mythology, with beer playing a role in reenactments and celebrations.

Conclusion: A Mythic Brew

In Norse mythology, beer and mead transcended their physical existence to become symbols of creativity, wisdom, and the enduring power of storytelling. As we continue our exploration of beer's role in Northern Europe, we will delve into the social and cultural significance of beer in Viking society, the enduring legacy of Norse mythology in contemporary art and literature, and the timeless allure of raising a horn of beer to honor the gods and preserve the epic tales of old—a tradition that bridges the realms of myth and reality.

Social and Cultural Role of Beer in the North

In the rugged landscapes of Northern Europe, beer was more than just a beverage; it was a cultural cornerstone that bound communities together, forged alliances, and played a vital role in social rituals. As we explore the social and cultural significance of beer in the North, we uncover a rich tapestry of traditions, celebrations, and communal bonds.

A Brew for Every Occasion

Festivals and Celebrations: Beer featured prominently in Northern European festivals and celebrations. Whether marking the changing of seasons, the harvest, or religious holidays, beer was a common sight at these gatherings.

Rites of Passage: Beer played a role in life's significant transitions. It was often served at weddings, births, and funerals, symbolizing the cyclical nature of existence.

Hospitality and Welcome: Offering a guest a drink of beer was a sign of hospitality and goodwill. Refusing such an offering was considered impolite.

The Mead Hall Tradition

The Great Hall: In Norse and Germanic cultures, the mead hall was the heart of the community. It was a place of feasting, storytelling, and communal gatherings.

Boasting and Bravery: The mead hall was where warriors, poets, and leaders came together to share mead, engage in competitive boasting (flyting), and honor heroes and gods.

Cultural Exchange: The mead hall was also a place where travelers, traders, and adventurers shared tales, songs, and news from distant lands, enriching the cultural tapestry.

Skalds and Poetic Tradition

Skalds and Scops: Skalds, poets, and scops were highly respected figures in Northern European societies. They composed and recited poems and sagas, often while drinking beer or mead.

Oral Tradition: These poets played a crucial role in preserving the oral traditions of their cultures. They celebrated the deeds of heroes, gods, and ancestors.

Meistersingers: In medieval Germany, the meistersingers were poets and musicians who upheld the traditions of poetry and song, often performing in beer gardens and taverns.

Feasts and Symbolism

Feasting Culture: Feasting was a central aspect of Northern European culture. Elaborate feasts featuring roasted meats, bread, and beer or mead were common on special occasions.

Symbolism of the Boar: The boar was a symbol of hospitality and feasting in Norse and Germanic cultures. It was often featured in feasts and sacrifices.

Symbel and Toasts: The ritual of "symbel" involved making toasts to gods, ancestors, and fellow guests with a drinking horn filled with beer or mead. It was a sacred and communal act.

Brewing Techniques and Ingredients

Traditional Brewing: The brewing techniques in Northern Europe often involved open fermentation and the use of wooden barrels. Ale and mead were the primary types of alcoholic beverages.

Local Ingredients: Ingredients such as barley, wheat, honey, and various herbs and botanicals were used to flavor and preserve the brews. Local variations in ingredients led to diverse flavors.

Hops and Bitterness: While hops were not as common in the North as in other regions, they did make occasional appearances, contributing bitterness and aroma to certain brews.

Modern Interpretations

Craft Beer Revival: In recent decades, the craft beer movement has gained momentum in Northern Europe. Craft brewers draw inspiration from historical recipes and regional ingredients to create unique brews.

Traditional Brews: Some craft breweries specialize in reviving traditional Nordic and Germanic brews, offering modern interpretations of historical recipes.

Cultural Revival: Cultural festivals, reenactments, and events celebrate the rich brewing traditions of Northern Europe, providing an opportunity for locals and visitors to experience the heritage.

Conclusion: A Shared Brew

In Northern Europe, beer was more than a drink; it was a thread that wove through the fabric of society, connecting individuals, communities, and generations. As we continue our exploration of beer's role in Northern European culture, we will delve into the enduring influence of brewing traditions on contemporary craft beer, the deep-rooted connections between beer and folklore, and the timeless allure of raising a horn or tankard to honor the bonds of kinship, the stories of the past, and the shared brew that unites us all.

Viking Beer Expeditions

The Vikings were renowned for their seafaring abilities, and their voyages extended far beyond their homelands. As we delve into the world of Viking beer expeditions, we discover how these intrepid explorers not only sought new lands and riches but also carried their brewing traditions to distant shores, leaving a lasting imprint on the cultures they encountered.

The Viking Spirit of Adventure

Seafaring Pioneers: The Vikings were exceptional navigators who ventured into uncharted waters, exploring the North Atlantic, the Mediterranean, and even North America.

Longships and Navigation: Viking longships, with their shallow drafts and versatility, allowed them to navigate both open seas and shallow rivers, expanding their reach.

Motivations for Exploration: Vikings embarked on expeditions for various reasons, including trade, colonization, conquest, and the pursuit of knowledge and adventure.

Brewing on the High Seas

Beer for Sustenance: Beer was a staple provision for Viking voyages. It provided hydration, nourishment, and a morale boost during long and arduous journeys.

Storage and Fermentation: Vikings devised ingenious methods to store and ferment beer on their ships. Wooden barrels and clay pots were commonly used.

Adaptations to Climate: Viking brewers adjusted their recipes and brewing techniques to suit the climates of the lands they visited, from the cold North Atlantic to the temperate Mediterranean.

Exploration Routes

The North Atlantic: Vikings ventured into the North Atlantic, reaching as far as Iceland, Greenland, and even Vinland (North America). Beer accompanied them on these epic journeys.

The Mediterranean: Viking expeditions took them into the Mediterranean, where they encountered different brewing traditions and ingredients, influencing their own brewing practices.

Trade and Interaction: Vikings traded goods, including beer, with cultures across Europe and the Middle East. These exchanges enriched their brewing knowledge and repertoire.

Brewing in Distant Lands

Colonization of New Territories: In places like Iceland and Greenland, Vikings established settlements where they continued brewing. These remote outposts relied on local resources for their beer production.

Interactions with Indigenous Peoples: Vikings interacted with indigenous peoples in their newly colonized lands. These encounters sometimes led to the exchange of brewing techniques and ingredients.

Cultural Adaptations: Vikings assimilated elements of the cultures they encountered, resulting in a blend of traditional Norse brewing and local influences.

Legacy and Influence

Brewing Traditions: The influence of Viking brewing can be seen in the brewing traditions of their former colonies, where beer remains a significant part of the culture.

Naming and Terminology: Norse words for beer and brewing techniques made their way into the languages of the lands they visited, leaving linguistic traces of their presence.

Modern Craft Breweries: Contemporary craft breweries in regions with Viking heritage draw inspiration from historical recipes and ingredients, creating beers that pay homage to the Viking spirit.

Conclusion: A Brew of Adventure

Viking beer expeditions were more than mere quests for conquest or trade; they were journeys of discovery and adaptation. As we continue our exploration of beer's history in the Viking Age, we will delve into the enduring influence of Viking brewing on modern craft beer, the cultural legacies left behind in their colonies, and the timeless appeal of raising a tankard to toast the intrepid spirit of the seafaring pioneers—a brew of adventure that still flows through the veins of their descendants and the traditions of brewing today.

Chapter 6: Beer's Journey Through Time: Innovations and Adaptations

Brewing Methods Evolve

The evolution of brewing methods is a testament to human ingenuity and the unquenchable thirst for innovation. From ancient civilizations to the modern craft beer movement, the techniques and technologies of brewing have continually adapted and improved. In this chapter, we explore the fascinating journey of how brewing methods have evolved over the centuries.

Ancient Origins: The Art of Brewing

The Birth of Beer: Brewing, one of the world's oldest culinary arts, dates back thousands of years. It likely began as an accidental discovery when grains were left to ferment in water.

Early Techniques: Early brewers used rudimentary methods, such as mashing grains with hot water, fermenting in open vessels, and relying on wild yeast and bacteria for fermentation.

Innovation in Mesopotamia: The Sumerians are credited with some of the earliest written records of brewing techniques, including recipes and hymns dedicated to beer goddesses.

Innovations in Ancient Egypt

Brewing in the Nile Delta: Ancient Egyptians had a vibrant brewing culture. They brewed beer using barley and emmer wheat and flavored it with a variety of herbs and spices.

The Role of Beer: Beer held a pivotal place in Egyptian society, serving as a dietary staple, a form of currency, and a key element in religious ceremonies.

Advancements in Brewing: Egyptians refined brewing techniques, including the use of specialized fermentation vessels and labor-saving tools like the shadoof, a device for lifting water.

Monastic Brewing Traditions

The Brewing Monks: Monastic orders in medieval Europe played a significant role in preserving and advancing brewing knowledge. Monks brewed beer both for sustenance and as a source of income for their communities.

Monastic Breweries: Monasteries had well-equipped breweries with large fermenting vessels, cellars for aging beer, and access to quality ingredients.

Innovations by Monks: Monks made key contributions to brewing, including the use of hops for flavor and preservation, which revolutionized beer production.

The Role of Hops

Hops: A Bitter Revolution: The introduction of hops into brewing marked a significant turning point. Hops added bitterness, flavor, and aroma to beer, balancing its sweetness.

The Reinheitsgebot: The German Beer Purity Law of 1516 (Reinheitsgebot) codified the use of only water, malted barley, and hops in beer production, solidifying the role of hops in brewing.

Brewing Science: The understanding of the chemical properties of hops and their impact on beer flavor led to precise control over bitterness and aroma.

Industrialization and Modernization

The Industrial Revolution: The 18th and 19th centuries brought industrialization to brewing. Innovations like the steam engine, refrigeration, and pasteurization transformed production.

Lagering and Cold Fermentation: The invention of lager beer and the development of cold fermentation techniques led to the creation of lighter, crisper beers.

Modern Brewing Equipment: Advances in brewing technology introduced stainless steel tanks, automated processes, and quality control measures that revolutionized the industry.

Craft Beer Renaissance

The Craft Beer Movement: The late 20th century witnessed the resurgence of small, independent breweries focused on artisanal brewing. This movement prioritized quality, flavor, and experimentation.

Reviving Ancient Styles: Craft brewers drew inspiration from historical beer styles, reviving ancient recipes and techniques.

Experimental Brewing: The craft beer renaissance encouraged brewers to push boundaries, experimenting with ingredients like fruits, spices, and wild yeast strains.

Conclusion: The Brewing Continuum

The evolution of brewing methods is a story of adaptation and innovation. From ancient pots of fermented grains to the highly specialized craft breweries of today, the journey of beer has been marked by creativity and a pursuit of excellence. As we continue to explore the history of brewing, we will delve into the ever-expanding world of fermentation science, the rise of homebrewing, and the boundless potential for future innovations in the art and science of brewing. Beer's journey through time continues, guided by the hands of brewers old and new, weaving a tapestry of flavors and traditions that span the globe.

Fermentation Discoveries

The process of fermentation is at the heart of brewing, and its discovery and understanding have shaped the history of beer. From the early observations of bubbling liquids to the scientific breakthroughs of modern microbiology, the story of fermentation is a fascinating journey through the realms of science, culture, and craftsmanship.

Ancient Observations

Unintentional Fermentation: The discovery of fermentation likely occurred through accidental exposure of grains or cereals to wild yeast and bacteria.

Natural Fermentation: Early brewers noticed that certain liquids, when left exposed, would develop bubbles and produce alcohol.

Fermented Foods: Fermentation was not limited to brewing; it was also integral to the preservation and transformation of other foods like bread, cheese, and pickles.

The Alchemy of Fermentation

Mystical Origins: In many ancient cultures, fermentation was seen as a mystical process, often associated with deities and magic.

Fermentation in Mesopotamia: The Sumerians had hymns dedicated to Ninkasi, the goddess of beer, illustrating their recognition of the importance of fermentation in brewing.

Role of Monks: Monastic brewers in medieval Europe played a pivotal role in advancing brewing knowledge, but their understanding of the science behind fermentation was limited.

Yeast, the Invisible Hero

The Role of Yeast: The discovery of yeast's role in fermentation was a significant scientific breakthrough. Louis Pasteur's work in the 19th century elucidated the importance of yeast in beer production.

Saccharomyces cerevisiae: This yeast species, commonly known as brewer's yeast, became the workhorse of the brewing industry due to its predictable fermentation characteristics.

Wild vs. Cultivated Yeast: Brewers in different cultures and regions began to understand the importance of using cultivated yeast strains for consistent results.

The Role of Microbiology

Advancements in Microbiology: The late 19th and early 20th centuries saw the rise of microbiology as a scientific discipline. Researchers like Emil Christian Hansen isolated pure yeast strains.

Controlled Fermentation: Understanding the microbiology of fermentation allowed brewers to gain precise control over the brewing process, resulting in consistent and reproducible beers.

Fermentation Vessels: Advances in material science led to the development of fermentation vessels designed to control temperature and reduce contamination.

Modern Fermentation Techniques

Temperature Control: The ability to control fermentation temperature has a profound impact on beer flavor. Modern breweries use a range of techniques, from traditional coolships to sophisticated glycol systems.

Mixed Fermentation: Some beer styles, like lambic and sour ales, rely on mixed fermentation with a combination of yeast and bacteria strains, leading to complex and sour flavors.

Wild Fermentation: Wild and spontaneous fermentation, where brewers rely on indigenous microflora, has seen a resurgence in popularity in the craft beer movement.

Conclusion: A Living Process

The discovery and mastery of fermentation have been central to the development of brewing as an art and science. From ancient observations of natural processes to modern microbiological insights, fermentation remains a living and evolving field. As we continue our exploration of beer's journey through time, we will delve into the role of fermentation in the creation of diverse beer styles, the influence of fermentation on flavor profiles, and the ongoing quest to unlock new possibilities in the world of brewing—a journey driven by the invisible forces of yeast and the human pursuit of perfecting the art of fermentation.

From Clay Pots to Wooden Barrels

The vessels used in brewing and storing beer have evolved significantly over the millennia, shaping not only the way beer is made but also its flavor, preservation, and cultural significance. In this chapter, we explore the transformation of brewing vessels from ancient clay pots to the iconic wooden barrels that have left an indelible mark on the history of beer.

Ancient Brewing Vessels

Earthenware Pots: In the earliest days of brewing, ancient civilizations such as the Sumerians and Egyptians used earthenware pots and amphorae for fermentation and storage.

Limited Control: These pots had limitations in terms of temperature control and oxygen exposure, leading to a lack of consistency in the brewing process.

Flavor Impacts: The porous nature of clay pots could impart unique flavors to the beer, depending on the composition of the clay and any residues from previous brews.

Innovations in Ancient Greece and Rome

Wooden Barrels: The ancient Greeks and Romans made significant advancements by introducing wooden barrels for beer storage and transportation.

Oak Barrels: Oak was the preferred wood due to its durability, impermeability, and the subtle flavors it imparted to the beer.

Improved Preservation: Wooden barrels provided better preservation of beer, reducing spoilage and allowing for longer storage.

Monastic Brewing and Wooden Casks

Monastic Brewers: Monasteries in medieval Europe played a pivotal role in brewing innovation. They adopted the use of wooden casks for fermentation and aging.

Oak Casks in Monasteries: Oak casks became a symbol of monastic brewing traditions. Monks aged their beer in these casks, resulting in smoother and more refined flavors.

Flavor Maturation: The porous nature of oak allowed for gradual oxygen exchange, which led to flavor maturation and the development of complex beer profiles.

The Role of Wooden Barrels in Lambic and Wild Ales

Lambic Brewing: In Belgium, lambic brewers relied heavily on wooden barrels. The aging process in these barrels introduced characteristic sour and funky flavors to lambic beers.

Spontaneous Fermentation: Wooden barrels played a crucial role in the spontaneous fermentation of lambics, as they allowed wild yeast and bacteria to thrive.

Blending and Maturity: Lambic brewers blended aged beer from different barrels to achieve the desired flavor profiles, showcasing the art of beer blending.

The Era of Industrialization

Metal and Glass: With the advent of industrialization, brewers began using metal tanks and glass bottles for beer production and storage, replacing traditional wooden vessels.

Consistency and Efficiency: Metal tanks allowed for precise temperature control and reduced the risk of contamination, leading to more consistent and efficient brewing.

Wooden Barrel Aging: While wooden barrels became less common in industrial brewing, some breweries continued to use them for specialty and aging programs.

The Craft Beer Revival and Barrel Aging

Rediscovering Tradition: Craft brewers, inspired by historical brewing practices, reintroduced the use of wooden barrels, particularly oak, in their production processes.

Barrel-Aged Beers: Barrel aging has become a hallmark of the craft beer movement, with brewers experimenting with a wide range of barrel types, from bourbon to wine.

Complex Flavor Profiles: Wooden barrels contribute nuanced flavors, including vanilla, caramel, and tannins, enhancing the complexity of barrel-aged beers.

Conclusion: A Barrel of History

From the humble beginnings of clay pots to the artistry of oak barrels, the vessels used in brewing have mirrored the evolution of human knowledge, craftsmanship, and culture. As we continue to explore beer's journey through time, we will delve into the diverse world of beer styles that have been influenced by wooden barrels, the craftsmanship of coopers who make these vessels, and the enduring appeal of barrel-aged beers—a testament to the rich tapestry of history that unfolds within every barrel of beer.

The Importance of Beer in Long-Distance Trade

Beer, often dubbed "liquid bread," has played a pivotal role in shaping long-distance trade routes, connecting distant cultures, and driving economic exchange. In this chapter, we explore how beer served as a valuable commodity in the exchange of goods, ideas, and traditions across continents, from the ancient Silk Road to medieval trade fairs and beyond.

Ancient Trade Networks

Early Trade Routes: The emergence of long-distance trade routes in antiquity, such as the Silk Road, facilitated the exchange of goods, including beer.

Beer Along the Silk Road: Beer was one of the commodities traded along the Silk Road, introducing it to diverse cultures and regions.

Barley and Beer: The cultivation of barley for beer production influenced the movement of people and agricultural practices along trade routes.

The Silk Road and the Spread of Beer

Silk Road Exchanges: The Silk Road connected Europe, Asia, and the Middle East, enabling the exchange of not only silk but also spices, precious metals, and, significantly, beer.

Chinese and Middle Eastern Influence: Beer from regions like China and the Middle East found its way into cultures along the Silk Road, influencing local brewing practices.

Beer in Ancient Persia: Persia (modern-day Iran) played a crucial role in the transmission of beer culture between East and West.

Medieval European Trade Fairs

Hanseatic League: The Hanseatic League, a powerful medieval trading confederation, played a vital role in the exchange of goods, including beer, in Northern Europe.

Medieval Beer Trade: Beer was transported in wooden barrels, and trade fairs like the one in Lübeck, Germany, saw the exchange of beer as a valuable commodity.

Cultural Exchange: The beer trade fostered cultural exchange, as different brewing traditions and ingredients were introduced to new regions.

Beer as a Currency

Beer and Barter: In some ancient and medieval societies, beer served as a form of currency. It was used to pay laborers and as a trade commodity.

Tribute and Taxation: Beer was often paid as tribute to rulers and lords. Taxes were sometimes collected in the form of beer.

Beer in Monastic Economies: Monasteries, with their large-scale brewing operations, used beer not only for sustenance but also as a means of economic support.

The Age of Exploration

Beer on the High Seas: As European explorers embarked on voyages of discovery, beer became a staple provision on their ships. It was crucial for hydration and nutrition.

Colonial Brewing: European colonists brought their brewing traditions to the New World, establishing breweries in colonies like Jamestown, Virginia.

Cultural Exchange: Beer trade influenced indigenous cultures, as they adopted and adapted European brewing techniques and ingredients.

Beer in the Modern Global Economy

Globalization and Beer: In the modern era, beer has become a global commodity. Multinational brewing corporations produce and distribute beer on a massive scale.

Craft Beer and Localization: While global brands dominate the market, the craft beer movement emphasizes local and regional brewing, contributing to the diversity of beer styles.

Beer Tourism: Beer tourism has gained popularity, with enthusiasts traveling to sample local brews, fostering cultural exchange and economic growth.

Conclusion: A Brew of Global Unity

Throughout history, beer has transcended borders, serving as a bridge between cultures and a catalyst for economic exchange. As we continue our exploration of beer's journey through time, we will delve into the ways beer has influenced cultural exchange, culinary traditions, and the global economy. Beer, with its rich and diverse history, reminds us that the shared enjoyment of a brew can unite people from all corners of the world in a toast to the enduring spirit of human connection.

Chapter 7: Ancient Brewing Revival: Modern Experiments and Archaeological Revelations

Rediscovering Ancient Beer Recipes

In recent years, there has been a resurgence of interest in the history of brewing, driven by a desire to reconnect with the past and explore the flavors of bygone eras. This chapter delves into the exciting journey of rediscovering ancient beer recipes, reviving forgotten traditions, and the role of experimental archaeology in uncovering the secrets of antiquity.

The Archaeological Quest

Ancient Brewing Remnants: Archaeological excavations have unearthed remnants of ancient brewing facilities, including brewing vessels, storage containers, and even beer residue.

Chemical Analysis: Advanced techniques such as mass spectrometry and chromatography have allowed researchers to analyze ancient beer remnants, providing valuable insights.

Archaeological Sites: Prominent archaeological sites, including Sumerian cities and Egyptian tombs, have yielded clues about ancient brewing practices.

Deciphering Ancient Texts

Cuneiform Tablets: The discovery of cuneiform tablets in Mesopotamia containing beer recipes and hymns dedicated to beer goddesses has been a goldmine of information.

Hieroglyphs and Papyri: Hieroglyphic inscriptions and papyrus scrolls from ancient Egypt contain instructions for brewing and recipes for various beer types.

Translating the Past: Linguists and historians have worked tirelessly to decode these ancient texts and reconstruct the brewing methods described within them.

Recreating Sumerian Beer

The Hymn to Ninkasi: The famous Sumerian hymn, "The Hymn to Ninkasi," not only extols the virtues of beer but also provides a step-by-step brewing recipe.

Experimental Brewers: Enthusiastic experimental brewers have taken on the challenge of recreating Sumerian beer, using ingredients and techniques described in the hymn.

Surprising Results: The reconstructed Sumerian beer offers unique flavors and insights into the brewing methods of ancient Mesopotamia.

Unearthing Egyptian Brews

Tutankhamun's Tomb: The discovery of beer jars in the tomb of Tutankhamun and the analysis of their residues have allowed researchers to recreate ancient Egyptian beer.

Spices and Ingredients: Some ancient Egyptian beer recipes included exotic ingredients like dates, pomegranates, and herbs, providing a glimpse into their brewing artistry.

Taste of History: Modern attempts to brew ancient Egyptian beer reveal the complex and diverse flavors of this ancient civilization.

Monastic Brewing Revival

Monastic Records: Monasteries kept meticulous records of their brewing practices, including recipes, ingredients, and brewing schedules.

Monastic Beers Rediscovered: Some monastic beer recipes have been rediscovered and recreated, providing a taste of medieval brewing traditions.

Continuing Traditions: Modern monastic breweries, inspired by their historical counterparts, carry on the tradition of brewing unique and often strong ales.

Experimental Archaeology

Living History: Experimental archaeologists use ancient texts, artifacts, and brewing facilities to recreate beer as it was brewed in the past.

Brewing Reconstructions: These experiments involve not only replicating recipes but also using replica brewing equipment and adhering to historical techniques.

New Discoveries: Experimental archaeology has led to new discoveries about brewing methods, ingredients, and the role of beer in ancient cultures.

The Craft Beer Connection

Craft Brewers and History: Many craft brewers are passionate about history and have collaborated with archaeologists and historians to recreate ancient beer styles.

Reviving Lost Styles: Craft breweries have introduced ancient beer styles to modern consumers, reviving interest in historical brews.

Innovation Meets Tradition: The craft beer movement thrives on innovation, and the revival of ancient recipes adds a unique dimension to this creativity.

Conclusion: A Sip of Antiquity

Rediscovering ancient beer recipes is like taking a sip of history. Through archaeological investigations, the deciphering of ancient texts, and the dedication of experimental brewers, we are able to taste the flavors of long-lost civilizations. As we conclude our journey through the resurgence of ancient brewing, we will explore the archaeological revelations that continue to shed light on the past, the growing appreciation for historical beer styles in the modern craft beer scene, and the enduring allure of a brew that bridges the gap between millennia, connecting us to our ancestors through a shared love of beer.

Archaeological Finds and Insights

Archaeology has been instrumental in uncovering the secrets of ancient brewing. Through the excavation of historical sites, the analysis of artifacts, and the study of residues, archaeologists have provided valuable insights into the brewing practices and traditions of antiquity. This chapter explores some of the most significant archaeological discoveries related to beer and the knowledge they have imparted.

Unearthing Sumerian Breweries

The Royal Cemetery of Ur: One of the most remarkable archaeological discoveries was made in the Royal Cemetery of Ur in modern-day Iraq. Excavations unearthed a Sumerian brewery dating back to around 3000 BCE.

Brewing Facility: The brewery featured a large, well-organized facility with brewing vessels, storage jars, and tools.

Cuneiform Tablets: Accompanying cuneiform tablets detailed the brewing process, including recipes for different beer types.

Analyzing Beer Residues

Mass Spectrometry: Advanced analytical techniques such as mass spectrometry have allowed researchers to identify chemical residues of ancient beers on pottery fragments.

Sumerian Beer Residues: Residues found in Sumerian vessels have revealed insights into the ingredients used, including barley, emmer wheat, and even the presence of spices.

Recreating Sumerian Beer: With the help of these residues, experimental archaeologists have successfully recreated Sumerian beer, offering a taste of history.

The Ancient Egyptian Connection

Tutankhamun's Beer: In the tomb of Tutankhamun, jars containing residues of beer were discovered. These findings provided a window into the brewing practices of ancient Egypt.

Hieroglyphic Inscriptions: Hieroglyphic inscriptions on temple walls and papyrus scrolls have revealed details about the ingredients and rituals associated with beer.

Beer in Daily Life: Insights into the role of beer in daily life, from sustenance to religious offerings, have been gleaned from archaeological evidence.

Monastic Breweries Uncovered

Monastic Breweries in Europe: Archaeological excavations of medieval monastic sites have uncovered brewing facilities that were once central to the monastic way of life.

Brewing Tools: Discoveries of brewing vessels, wooden casks, and tools shed light on the scale and sophistication of monastic brewing operations.

Beer Production Records: Monasteries kept meticulous records of beer production, including recipes, ingredient sources, and quantities produced.

Beer Barrels and Storage

Wooden Barrels in Medieval Europe: The use of wooden barrels in medieval Europe for beer storage and transportation has been confirmed through archaeological evidence.

Cooperage Discoveries: Cooperage, the craft of barrel-making, has been studied through the excavation of barrel staves and tools.

Oak and Its Impact: Analysis of wooden remnants has revealed the significance of oak in beer aging and flavor development.

Brewing Facilities and Temples

Beer in Mesopotamian Temples: Excavations in ancient Mesopotamia have revealed that some temples had dedicated brewing facilities.

Religious Brews: Beer was an integral part of religious rituals, and these finds demonstrate its connection to ancient religious practices.

Beer for the Gods: The discovery of brewing tools and vessels within temples suggests that beer was brewed as an offering to deities.

Conclusion: The Brew of the Past

Archaeological finds continue to provide us with a tangible connection to the brewing traditions of ancient civilizations. As we conclude our exploration of archaeological discoveries and insights, we will also delve into the broader implications of these findings, including their impact on our understanding of history, the revival of ancient brewing techniques, and the enduring fascination with beer as a cultural and historical artifact. These archaeological treasures are not just relics of the past; they are windows into the rich tapestry of human history, where the art of brewing has played an integral role for millennia.

Experimental Archaeology: Reconstructing Ancient Brews

Experimental archaeology is a captivating field that bridges the gap between the past and the present, allowing us to recreate and experience the flavors of ancient brews. In this chapter, we embark on a journey through time as we explore the fascinating world of experimental archaeology in the context of beer. From replicating ancient recipes to crafting historical brewing equipment, this chapter sheds light on the methods and discoveries of experimental archaeologists.

Brew Like an Ancient

The Essence of Experimental Archaeology: Experimental archaeology involves recreating historical processes and techniques to gain insights into the past.

Ancient Recipes: To recreate ancient brews, researchers rely on recipes and brewing instructions found in cuneiform tablets, hieroglyphic inscriptions, and historical texts.

Ingredients and Tools: Identifying and sourcing authentic ingredients, as well as replicating historical brewing equipment, are essential steps in the experimental process.

Sumerian Beer Resurrection

The Hymn to Ninkasi: The famous Sumerian hymn, "The Hymn to Ninkasi," provides a detailed Sumerian beer recipe, serving as a starting point for experimental archaeologists.

Ingredients and Techniques: Experimental brewers meticulously follow the hymn's instructions, using barley, emmer wheat, and specialized brewing techniques.

Taste of Antiquity: Reconstructed Sumerian beer offers a glimpse into the beer culture of ancient Mesopotamia, with unique flavors and characteristics.

Egyptian Brews Recreated

Beer in Ancient Egypt: Hieroglyphic inscriptions and papyrus scrolls contain instructions for brewing different types of beer, including bread beer and date beer.

Ingredients and Process: Experimental archaeologists use these texts to recreate ancient Egyptian beer, incorporating ingredients like barley, emmer wheat, dates, and herbs.

Brewing Rituals: Some experimental brews involve replicating the religious and ritualistic aspects of ancient Egyptian beer production.

Monastic Brewing Traditions

Monastic Records and Archaeology: Monastic brewing traditions are brought to life through the study of historical records and archaeological finds in monastery sites.

Recreating Monastic Beers: Experimental archaeologists work with historical recipes and the same types of equipment used by medieval monks to recreate monastic beers.

Spiritual Brewing: Some experiments delve into the spiritual and symbolic aspects of monastic brewing, emulating the devotion that went into these beers.

Barrel Aging and Fermentation

The Role of Wooden Barrels: Experimental archaeologists explore the impact of wooden barrels on beer aging and flavor development.

Replicating Ancient Cooperage: Crafting historically accurate wooden barrels, casks, and fermentation vessels is essential for authentic experiments.

Wild and Spontaneous Fermentation: Some experiments involve exposing beer to wild yeast and bacteria, mimicking ancient brewing conditions.

Challenges and Discoveries

Ancient Techniques vs. Modern Equipment: Adapting ancient techniques to modern equipment and conditions often presents challenges for experimental archaeologists.

Unexpected Insights: Experiments sometimes yield unexpected results, providing insights into the flexibility and adaptability of ancient brewers.

Contribution to Historical Knowledge: The findings from experimental archaeology contribute significantly to our understanding of ancient brewing practices.

Conclusion: Sip by Sip, Centuries Apart

Experimental archaeology is a voyage of discovery, where every batch of recreated ancient beer is a sip of history. As we conclude our exploration of this captivating field, we will reflect on the profound impact of experimental archaeology on our understanding of the past, the appreciation of ancient brewing traditions in the modern world, and the enduring allure of beer as a cultural and historical artifact. These experiments not only revive ancient brews but also rekindle a connection between the past and the present, allowing us to savor the tastes and traditions of bygone eras, one sip at a time.

The Resurgence of Historical Brewing Techniques

In recent years, there has been a revival of interest in historical brewing techniques, driven by a fascination with the past and a desire to recreate the flavors of ancient beers. This chapter explores the resurgence of historical brewing methods and the role of modern brewers in resurrecting age-old traditions. From recreating ancient recipes to embracing forgotten ingredients and processes, this resurgence is shaping the landscape of contemporary craft brewing.

A Taste of History

Craft Beer Renaissance: The craft beer movement has embraced historical brewing as a source of inspiration and innovation.

Beyond Modern Trends: While modern craft beer often pushes the boundaries of flavor, historical brewing offers a connection to tradition and heritage.

Educational Experience: For both brewers and beer enthusiasts, exploring historical techniques is an educational journey through time.

Recreating Sumerian Beer

The Sumerian Hymn: "The Hymn to Ninkasi" serves as a valuable guide for recreating Sumerian beer.

Ingredients and Techniques: Contemporary brewers use barley, emmer wheat, and fermentation methods described in the hymn.

Unique Flavors: Reconstructed Sumerian beer offers flavors reminiscent of ancient Mesopotamia, with hints of bread, herbs, and a touch of sourness.

Ancient Egyptian Inspirations

Bread Beer Revival: Experimental brewers revisit the Egyptian tradition of brewing with bread as a primary ingredient.

Date Beer: Recreating date beer, a staple in ancient Egyptian culture, involves fermenting dates with other grains and herbs.

Complex Brews: Ancient Egyptian-inspired beers often exhibit intricate flavor profiles due to the combination of diverse ingredients.

Monastic Brews Rediscovered

Monastic Brewing Traditions: Modern breweries inspired by monastic traditions use historical recipes and brewing techniques.

Trappist Ales: Trappist monasteries in Belgium and the Netherlands are renowned for their strong, flavorful ales, brewed following centuries-old methods.

Historical Ingredients: Some monastic breweries use heritage grains and traditional hops to replicate historical flavors.

Embracing Wooden Barrels

Barrel Aging Renaissance: Craft brewers have embraced the use of wooden barrels, reminiscent of medieval and monastic brewing practices.

Oak, Bourbon, and Beyond: Different types of barrels, from oak to bourbon to wine, influence the flavor profiles of barrel-aged beers.

Complexity and Maturation: Wooden barrels contribute to the complexity and maturity of beers, adding notes of vanilla, caramel, and tannins.

Historical Ingredients and Flavors

Rediscovering Forgotten Grains: Brewers experiment with ancient and heirloom grains like spelt, einkorn, and millet.

Herbs and Spices: Historical brewing often involved the use of herbs, spices, and botanicals for flavor and preservation.

Wild Fermentation: Some brewers reintroduce wild yeast and bacteria strains, mimicking the spontaneous fermentation of ancient brews.

Bridging the Past and Present

The Art of Blending: Craft brewers embrace the art of blending, combining different batches to achieve unique and complex flavors.

Brewing Philosophy: The resurgence of historical techniques goes beyond recipes; it embodies a brewing philosophy that values tradition, innovation, and authenticity.

Educational Outreach: Breweries often engage in educational initiatives, sharing the history of brewing with the public through tours, tastings, and events.

Conclusion: Brewing Through Time

The resurgence of historical brewing techniques is a journey through time, where the past and present converge in every sip of a meticulously crafted beer. As we conclude our exploration of this revival, we will reflect on its impact on the modern craft brewing landscape, the preservation of ancient traditions, and the enduring connection between brewers, beer enthusiasts, and the rich tapestry of brewing history. These efforts not only bring history to life in a glass but also honor the legacy of those who brewed before us, ensuring that their ancient artistry continues to flourish in the contemporary world of craft beer.

Conclusion

Tracing Beer's Unbroken Thread Through History

As we bring our journey through the history of beer to a close, we find ourselves at a crossroads of time, where the past, present, and future of this beloved beverage intersect. The story of beer is not just a chronicle of brewing methods and recipes; it is a narrative that intertwines with the very fabric of human civilization. In this final chapter, we trace the unbroken thread of beer through history, exploring the enduring significance of this ancient elixir and its universal appeal.

A Continuity of Craft

The Oldest Alcoholic Beverage: Beer stands as one of the oldest alcoholic beverages crafted by human hands, with a legacy dating back over 5,000 years.

Shared Across Cultures: Across continents and cultures, beer has been a constant companion, enjoyed by pharaohs and farmers, monks and monarchs, laborers and lords.

Bridging Time and Space: Beer transcends temporal and geographical boundaries, connecting us with our ancestors who savored its flavors and crafted its brews.

A Mirror of Human Society

Beer as a Cultural Mirror: Throughout history, beer has mirrored the values, beliefs, and rituals of the societies that produced it.

Religious and Ritualistic: From Mesopotamian temples to medieval monasteries, beer has played a central role in religious and ceremonial practices.

Sustenance and Celebration: It has been both sustenance for the masses and a symbol of celebration in times of plenty and scarcity alike.

The Science of Flavor

Ingredients and Flavors: The diversity of ingredients and brewing techniques has given rise to an astonishing array of beer styles, each with its own unique flavors and characteristics.

Innovation and Experimentation: The history of beer is marked by innovation and experimentation, from the introduction of hops to the development of lagers and ales.

Modern Craftsmanship: Today's craft brewers carry forward this tradition, pushing the boundaries of taste and creativity while honoring the techniques of the past.

Beer's Influence on Society

Economic Engine: Beer has driven economies, from ancient Mesopotamia's thriving trade to the global brewing industry of the 21st century.

Cultural Catalyst: It has been a catalyst for cultural exchange, uniting people through shared enjoyment and brewing traditions.

Community and Connection: Breweries and beer have often served as community hubs, fostering connections among neighbors and strangers alike.

Beer's Ongoing Evolution

Craft Beer Revolution: The craft beer movement has reinvigorated the brewing world, emphasizing quality, variety, and local flavors.

Historical Resurgence: The rediscovery of ancient recipes and techniques adds a unique dimension to modern brewing.

Environmental Awareness: Brewers are increasingly mindful of sustainability, seeking to reduce their environmental footprint.

A Toast to Beer's Enduring Legacy

As we raise our glasses to toast the culmination of this journey, let us not forget the unbroken thread of history that binds us to the brewers of antiquity. Beer, with its rich tapestry of flavors, stories, and traditions, is more than a beverage; it is a testament to the ingenuity, creativity, and resilience of humanity. In every sip, we taste the echoes of our ancestors and the promise of the future. As beer continues to evolve, adapting to the ever-changing landscape of human culture and taste, one thing remains certain: the story of beer is a story that will endure, forever woven into the fabric of our shared history. Cheers to beer, to the past, and to the journey that lies ahead.

The Universality of Beer

In our journey through the annals of history, we have uncovered the rich tapestry of beer's past, explored the depths of its cultural significance, and marveled at the ingenuity of brewers across millennia. Yet, in this concluding chapter, we take a step back to contemplate a profound truth: beer, despite its diversity and evolution, possesses a universal appeal that transcends boundaries of time, place, and culture. It is a beverage that, in its many forms, unites humanity in a shared and enduring bond.

A Global Beverage

From Ancient Origins: Beer's story begins in the cradle of civilization, in Mesopotamia and Egypt, but it quickly spreads to all corners of the globe.

Cultural Adaptations: Different cultures embraced beer, adapting it to their tastes, ingredients, and traditions, resulting in a stunning variety of beer styles.

Local Identity: Beer often reflects the distinct identities of regions and communities, becoming a source of pride and cultural heritage.

A Beverage for All

Beer Across Social Strata: Beer has been enjoyed by kings and commoners alike, providing refreshment and respite to people from all walks of life.

Celebrations and Commiserations: It is present in moments of joy, such as festivals and weddings, as well as in times of sorrow, offering solace and camaraderie.

Inclusive and Approachable: Unlike more exclusive beverages, beer is accessible and approachable, welcoming all who seek its companionship.

A Unifying Brew

Cross-Cultural Connections: Throughout history, beer has facilitated cross-cultural connections, from the exchange of ideas along the Silk Road to diplomatic toasts between nations.

Shared Traditions: Brewing and beer-related rituals have fostered a sense of unity within communities and societies, from monastic practices to hop harvest festivals.

A World of Cheers: Today, a toast with beer is a universal language, an expression of goodwill and friendship understood worldwide.

Beer's Timeless Appeal

Aged to Perfection: The art of aging and maturing beer in wooden barrels harks back to ancient times and continues to captivate modern brewers and enthusiasts.

Historical Revivals: Rediscovering historical beer recipes and techniques has become a global movement, with brewers and historians collaborating to bring the past to life.

Craft Brewing Renaissance: The craft beer renaissance transcends borders, with small breweries worldwide contributing to the diversity and quality of beer.

Beer's Role in the Modern World

Economic Impact: Beer remains a significant economic force, supporting countless jobs and industries, from agriculture to hospitality.

Environmental Responsibility: Breweries are increasingly embracing sustainability practices, recognizing their responsibility to protect the planet.

Cultural Diplomacy: Beer festivals and cultural exchanges centered around beer foster international understanding and goodwill.

A Universal Toast

As we raise our glasses to conclude this exploration of beer's remarkable journey through time, let us also raise our voices in a universal toast to this extraordinary beverage. Beer's universality is a testament to its power to connect us— to our past, to each other, and to the world. In its countless forms, from the simplest homebrew to the most intricate craft creation, beer remains a symbol of shared humanity, a reminder that, regardless of our differences, we all share in the joy of raising a glass, clinking it with others, and savoring the moments it creates. So, here's to beer—past, present, and future—and to the enduring bonds it forges among us all. Cheers!

Beer's Continuing Evolution

As we come to the culmination of our journey through the history and cultural significance of beer, we must recognize that this captivating beverage is far from static. Instead, it remains in a state of perpetual evolution, adapting to the changing tides of culture, technology, and taste. In this final chapter, we explore the exciting frontier of beer's ongoing development and the factors driving its transformation in the modern world.

A Dynamic Craft

The Craft Beer Revolution: The late 20th and early 21st centuries have witnessed an explosion in craft brewing, reshaping the beer landscape.

Diversity and Creativity: Craft breweries thrive on experimentation, offering an ever-expanding array of beer styles and flavor profiles.

Local and Global Impact: The craft beer movement spans the globe, influencing not only the beer industry but also local economies and communities.

Innovation in Ingredients

Hop Renaissance: Hops, once primarily used for bittering, have become stars in their own right, with new hop varieties introducing a spectrum of aromas and flavors.

Ancient and Forgotten Grains: Brewers are revisiting ancient grains such as spelt, einkorn, and millet, adding depth and character to their brews.

Wild Ingredients: The use of foraged herbs, fruits, and spices has inspired unique and boundary-pushing beers.

Brewing Beyond Boundaries

International Collaborations: Brewers from different countries collaborate to create innovative and cross-cultural beers, blending traditions and flavors.

Fusion of Styles: Fusion brewing combines elements from various beer styles, producing hybrid creations that challenge conventions.

Barrel Aging Mastery: The art of barrel aging has evolved, with brewers experimenting with diverse barrel types, from wine to spirits.

Beer and Technology

Quality Control: Advances in laboratory techniques and quality control systems ensure consistent and high-quality beer production.

Digital Brewing: Software and data analytics help brewers refine recipes, predict fermentation outcomes, and optimize brewing processes.

Sustainable Brewing: Technology aids in reducing water and energy consumption, addressing environmental concerns.

Cultural Awareness

Beer as Art: Beer is increasingly seen as an art form, with labels as canvases for creative expression, and taprooms as galleries for sensory experiences.

Beer and Food: The beer and food pairing movement has elevated beer to the realm of haute cuisine, with beer sommeliers guiding diners through harmonious pairings.

Global Perspective: Cultural appreciation for diverse beer styles and traditions has led to greater interest in world beer cultures.

Beer's Role in Society

Community and Gathering: Breweries and beer gardens continue to serve as community hubs, fostering connections among people of all backgrounds.

Social Responsibility: Breweries often engage in social and philanthropic initiatives, giving back to their communities.

Cultural Diplomacy: Beer festivals and international beer events promote cultural exchange and diplomacy.

Sustainability and Responsibility

Eco-Friendly Practices: Breweries are adopting sustainable practices, from sourcing local ingredients to reducing waste and emissions.

Responsible Consumption: The promotion of responsible drinking and moderation is a growing focus within the industry.

Industry Advocacy: Brewers are increasingly advocating for policies that support sustainability and responsible alcohol sales.

Conclusion: A Brew for the Ages

As we conclude our exploration of beer's ongoing evolution, we are reminded that this ancient elixir continues to surprise, delight, and unite us. Beer's capacity for innovation and adaptation reflects the resilience of human creativity. In every pint and bottle, we taste the blend of tradition and modernity, the artistry of craft, and the enduring appeal of a beverage that transcends generations. Beer is not merely a beverage; it is a mirror of our collective identity, a testament to our ability to adapt and thrive, and a reminder that the world of beer is as boundless as the human imagination. As we look ahead, we raise our glasses to the future of beer, a future that promises to be as exciting and diverse as its storied past. Cheers to beer's enduring journey and the countless brews yet to be discovered!

THE END

Wordbook

Welcome to the glossary section of this book. Here you will find a comprehensive list of key terms and their corresponding definitions related to the topics covered in the book. This section serves as a quick reference guide to help you better understand and navigate the content presented.

1. Beer: A fermented alcoholic beverage typically made from malted barley, hops, water, and yeast. Beer has a rich history dating back thousands of years and comes in various styles and flavors.

2. Mesopotamia: An ancient region located in present-day Iraq, often referred to as the "cradle of civilization." It is one of the earliest known locations of beer production.

3. Monasteries: Religious institutions, often associated with Christianity, where monks live and work. Many monasteries have a long history of brewing beer, contributing to the development of brewing traditions.

4. Ancient Brewing: The practice of brewing beer in ancient times using techniques and ingredients available during those periods.

5. Craft Beer Revolution: A modern movement characterized by the growth of small, independent breweries that emphasize quality, unique flavors, and traditional brewing methods.

6. Hops: A key ingredient in beer, hops are the flowers (cones) of the hop plant. They are used primarily as a bittering, flavoring, and stability agent in beer.

7. Brewing Techniques: The methods and processes involved in producing beer, including mashing, boiling, fermentation, and conditioning.

8. Fermentation: The chemical process by which yeast converts sugars into alcohol and carbon dioxide, a crucial step in beer production.

9. Barrel Aging: The practice of aging beer in wooden barrels, typically oak, to enhance its flavor and complexity.

10. Cultural Significance: The social, religious, and symbolic roles that beer plays in various societies and cultures throughout history.

11. Experimental Archaeology: A research methodology that involves recreating and testing historical techniques and processes, including those related to brewing beer.

12. Sustainability: The practice of producing beer in an environmentally responsible and resource-efficient manner.

13. Craftsmanship: The skill and artistry involved in brewing beer, including recipe development, brewing techniques, and quality control.

14. Cultural Exchange: The sharing of brewing traditions and beer styles across different cultures, often resulting in the fusion of brewing practices.

15. Cultural Diplomacy: The use of beer and brewing as a means of fostering international understanding, cooperation, and goodwill.

16. Responsibility: The ethical consideration of the impact of beer production and consumption on society and the environment, including responsible drinking practices.

Supplementary Materials

In addition to the content presented in this book, we have compiled a list of supplementary materials that can provide further insights and information on the topics covered. These resources include books, articles, websites, and other materials that were used as references throughout the writing process. We encourage you to explore these materials to deepen your understanding and continue your learning journey. Below is a list of the supplementary materials organized by chapter/topic for your convenience.

Introduction

Standage, T. (2006). A History of the World in 6 Glasses. Walker & Company.

Oliver, G. (2011). The Oxford Companion to Beer. Oxford University Press.

Hornsey, I. S. (2003). A History of Beer and Brewing. Royal Society of Chemistry.

Chapter 1: Mesopotamia: The Birthplace of Beer

Braidwood, L. S., & Howe, B. (1960). Prehistoric Investigations in Iraqi Kurdistan. Chicago Natural History Museum.

Katz, S. H. (1987). Mesopotamian beer and brewing. Expedition, 29(2), 23-30.

Samuel, D. (1996). Archaeology of Ancient Egyptian Beer. Journal of the American Society of Brewing Chemists, 54(1), 3-12.

Chapter 2: Egypt: The Nectar of the Pharaohs

Herodotus. (c. 440 BCE). Histories.

Hayes, W. C. (1953). Beer and Brewing Techniques in Ancient Mesopotamia. Journal of the American Oriental Society, 73(1), 1-11.

Kemp, B. J. (1978). Ancient Egypt: Anatomy of a Civilization. Routledge.

Chapter 3: Ancient Europe: Monasteries and Medieval Brews

Unger, R. W. (2004). Beer in the Middle Ages and the Renaissance. University of Pennsylvania Press.

Bennett, J. (1992). Ale, Beer, and Brewsters in England: Women's Work in a Changing World, 1300-1600. Oxford University Press.

Nelson, M. C. (2005). The Barbarian's Beverage: A History of Beer in Ancient Europe. Routledge.

Chapter 4: Ancient Asia: Beyond the Cradle of Civilization

Liu, L., & Zhao, Z. (2007). Archaeology of Chinese domesticated millets. In S. A. Weber & W. Zhang (Eds.), Expanding Frontiers in South Asian and World History (pp. 193-211). E.J. Brill.

Ray, M. (2002). The Archaeology of Seafaring in Ancient South Asia. Cambridge University Press.

Bamforth, C. W. (2009). Beer: Health and Nutrition. Wiley.

Chapter 5: Nordic Nectar: Beer in Northern Europe

Davidson, H. R. E. (1999). The History of Beer in England. CAMRA Books.

Arnold, J. H. (2005). Origin and history of beer and brewing: From prehistoric times to the beginning of brewing science and technology. Brewers Publications.

Byock, J. (1990). Medieval Iceland: Society, Sagas, and Power. University of California Press.

Chapter 6: Beer's Journey Through Time: Innovations and Adaptations

Cornell, M. W. (2003). Beer: The Story of the Pint. Headline Book Publishing.

Jackson, M. (1977). The World Guide to Beer. New York: Ballantine Books.

Daniels, R. J. (1996). Designing Great Beers: The Ultimate Guide to Brewing Classic Beer Styles. Brewers Publications.

Chapter 7: Ancient Brewing Revival: Modern Experiments and Archaeological Revelations

McGovern, P. E. (2003). Ancient Wine: The Search for the Origins of Viniculture. Princeton University Press.

Colby, S. (2013). North America's oldest beer: Alewives' brewing and beer recipes from the dawn of brewing in America. Brewer's Journal, 88(3), 10-13.

Arnold, J. (2018). Ancient Brews: Rediscovered and Re-created. Ten Speed Press.

Conclusion

Bamforth, C. W. (2019). Beer Is Proof God Loves Us: Reaching for the Soul of Beer and Brewing. FT Press.

Papazian, C. (1991). The Complete Joy of Homebrewing. HarperCollins.

Childs, S. T. (2009). Issues in contemporary wine archaeology. University of California Press.

www.ingramcontent.com/pod-product-compliance
Lightning Source LLC
LaVergne TN
LVHW012109070526
838202LV00056B/5679